COMMAND

THE
PHILADELPHIA
EXPERIMENT
CHRONICLES

Exploring The Strange Case of
Alfred Bielek & Dr. M.K. Jessup

ABELARD PRODUCTIONS, INC.

Contents

Introduction

Being a one-time active Commander in the military (I still choose to leave my "rank and serial number" out of all this), I've long been intrigued with any and all speculation about the Philadelphia Experiment, which included aspects of invisibility, time travel, and the possible interference of an alien intelligence in our technical development.

A highly classified—Above Top Secret—project conducted by the Navy in 1943, the Philadelphia Experiment involved the teleportation of the *U.S.S. Eldridge* (a mega-ton destroyer) from its dry dock in the Philadelphia Naval Yard to Norfolk, Virginia —a distance of around 400 miles.

During at least part of the time, the *Eldridge* was "missing" from the City of Brotherly Love, the destroyer was said to have been transported into another dimension—a sort of no man's land of darkness and silence from which few have been known to come back. Indeed, upon returning to this *time and space,* most of the vessel's crew—all of whom had been left totally unprepared and unprotected by those scientists put in charge of the project—either "caught on fire," got literally frozen into the hull of the ship, or went stark, raving mad.

Those who were "lucky," and appeared to return to some semblance of normality after the experiment was officially shut down, soon found themselves living a hellish existence as they were repeatedly pulled back into this *alternate reality* to relive the horrors of the Philadelphia Experiment over and over again —until there were only two survivors left in the world.

Depressed!
Demented!

Driven utterly insane!

One by one, those who remained *with us* found themselves fighting a brand new enemy—our own government. Much like the use of Agent Orange in Vietnam and more recently with nerve gas employed by the enemy in the Gulf War, our own leaders tried their damnest to cover their own tracks. Refusing to acknowledge any responsibility for their own actions, it has seemingly become policy to deny any involvement or wrong-doing in such matters. The same was apparently true back in 1943 with the Philadelphia Experiment. Indeed, the government has tried to make the public believe that such wartime "incidents" never really happened—that they are simply the product of overactive imaginations or the mumblings of professional conspiracy buffs.

Now we know better!

We now know for SURE that the Philadelphia Experiment *really* did take place.

Little by little over the years, we have managed to pull together pieces of a great puzzle. Two mass market books have already been published on the subject (*The Philadelphia Experiment* by Charles Berlitz and William Moore, and *The Philadelphia Experiment and Other UFO Conspiracies* by Brad and Sherry Steiger); countless confidential monographs have been issued by legitimate researchers; and at least two major motion pictures have been based on what took place back then.

In essence, you might say that the cover-up has failed!

So why are we being left in the dark about a matter that might possibly provide us with so much technological data and information that could—in the long run—be of tremendous advantage to each and every one of us?

How could it be that our loved ones have died on the battlefields for a country that refuses to reveal to us the plain and simple facts we so actively seek? Why, indeed, is it necessary for us to be fed such illogical misinformation and downright lies when our Constitution is supposed to guarantee us so much more?

I am so glad to be able to rip away the wall of secrecy and silence that surrounds the Philadelphia Experiment, and allow those of us who honestly seek the truth to know exactly what happened in this tragic matter.

In the pages that follow, you will be introduced to individuals that you may not be altogether familiar with. As we go along, I will be writing about the likes of Alfred Bielek, Dr. Morris K. Jessup, Gray Barker, Riley Crabb, and the very enigmatic Carlos Allende who—for all intents and purposes—set us on the right track, despite his peculiar, highly unorthodox behavior that, upon first examination, might tend to turn a lot of us off.

To my own contacts in the military who have led me to certain vital documents, and to the efforts of several independent investigators who have refused to "give up the ship" (and may have later died under mysterious circumstances because they knew too much), we all owe a world of thanks.

Maybe after reading *The Philadelphia Experiment Chronicles* you will be able to sleep just a bit better at night, knowing that the truth has finally came out.

I certainly hope so.

Commander X

Philadelphia Newspaper Story
circa mid 1940s

Strange Circumstances
Surround Tavern Brawl

Several city police officers responding to a call to aid members of the Navy Shore Patrol in breaking up a tavern brawl near the U.S. Navy docks here last night got something of a surprise when they arrived on the scene to find the place empty of customers. According to a pair of very nervous waitresses, the Shore Patrol had arrived first and cleared the place out—but not before two of the sailors involved allegedly did a disappearing act. "They just sort of vanished into thin air, right there," reported one of the frightened hostesses, "and I ain't been drinking either!" At that point, according to her account, the Shore Patrol proceeded to hustle everyone out of the place in short order.

A subsequent chat with the local police precinct left no doubts as to the fact that some sort of general brawl had indeed occurred in the vicinity of the dockyards at about eleven o'clock last night, but neither confirmation nor denial of the stranger aspects of the story could be immediately obtained. One reported witness succinctly summed up the affair by dismissing it as nothing more than "A lot of hooey from them daffy dames down there." Who, he went on to say, were just looking for some free publicity.

Damage to the tavern was estimated to be in the vicinity of six hundred dollars.

Those involved in the Philadelphia Experiment insist Albert Einstein was one of the major scientific forces who set up the project. Here Einstein is seen with Navy top brass in his library in Princeton, New Jersey.

Chapter One
The Strange Case of
Dr. Morris K. Jessup

There is so much to tell that it is difficult to decide where to begin.

There is now a large reservoir of information at our disposal to prove once and for all that the Philadelphia Experiment was not some post World War II hallucination caused by the madness of the situation or the development of the atomic bomb.

Gray Barker was a long time researcher on the Philadelphia Experiment. Residing almost all of his life in the Clarksburg, West Virginia area, the six-foot-six author of such works as *They Knew Too Much About Flying Saucers,* and *The Silver Bridge,* loved a good mystery. Editor for many years of *The Saucerian Bulletin,* Barker first got into UFOlogy about 1950, when a strange creature with glowing eyes appeared in front of several eyewitnesses, seemingly floating above the ground and giving off a terrible stench. After finding unexplained, strange markings in the soil nearby, Barker came away convinced that an alien craft had landed in the rural town of Flatwoods, West Virginia, and that some sort of interplanetary invasion was underway.

One of Barker's earliest correspondents and associates was an astronomer by the name of Dr. Morris K. Jessup, who wrote a series of articles for *The Saucerian Bulletin,* and later some best-selling UFO books.

Both Gray Barker and Dr. Jessup are now deceased. In all

There is now evidence that the late Dr. M.K. Jessup died because he stumbled upon the truth about the Philadelphia Experiment and the Allende Letters.

probability, Barker's death was not related to anything connected with UFOs or the Philadelphia Experiment. We cannot in all honesty say the same for the astronomer who ended up sacrificing both his career and his life due to what he discovered about the Philadelphia Experiment. Maybe we're better off letting Mr. Barker tell the full story, since Jessup was his friend and a contributor to his publication.

• • •

Early Writings of Dr. Jessup

I first had contact with Jessup on November 5, 1954, shortly after I sent him an issue of my publication, *The Saucerian*, and shortly before his first book was published. Here is a part of his reply:

"Thanks for your letter of the 4th rec this morning. And thanks to J. Bessor for sending you my name. I have another copy of *The Saucerian* which John loaned to me (Vol. II, No. II) and must say that you are doing a real job with it. The labor alone of turning out all that copy must be tremendous.

"Yes, I'm doing a book. It is far along in the final draft stages, and we are hoping to get it in the hands of the publishers sometime next week. It is rather conservative as compared to some of the wild things so far printed, but I have tried to keep it factual, and have confined it to phenomena in the pre-Arnold era—particularly around 1875–1885. Altogether it makes quite a formidable array of proof and background.

"I am hoping to market it, in part, through the Library Research Group which is a company being set up for selling books. I will want to advertise it through such publications as yours, when the time comes, but not until after I have a contract with the publishers, which will be at least two to three weeks yet. As soon as I have the contract I will send you some kind of release.

"I used to drive through Clarksburg fairly often, visiting relatives in Indiana, but haven't been through there for almost two years now. If I get out that way I'll drop in and see you. Meanwhile, if you're over this way, drop in. I always have time to talk about saucer problems."

Correspondence continued between Jessup and myself, and I quote some of it mainly to demonstrate something of the personality of the author. He was a most cordial person, and greatly enthusiastic about finding some solution to the UFO mystery—though he indicated that in his professional writing he felt it necessary to take a more conservative approach. This conservative, scientific attitude, demonstrated in his first two books, may have been the reason that his writings were not popular with many saucer "fans."

"There is so damned much nonsense (he wrote on December 16, 1954) being put out by silly people that one gets disgusted with a lot of it. I do feel that we are in a remarkable phase of human experience and that the waters should not be muddied by stupidity—the problem is tough enough without any Adamskis in the picture.

"You mention wanting material (I had requested articles for *The Saucerian*—G.B.). What do you want most? I am not as much in touch with current reports as are most of your readers but I go heavy on the scientific approach. I would be glad to write a page or two for you, and if you wish I would be glad to act (gratis) as Astronomical Consultant, if it would be of any value to you.

"I think I could do a page regarding the motive power of the UFO stressing the point that the rocket and magnetic drives are impractical. Later when the book is out I can spread out a bit, but right now I don't want to release too many unpublished ideas."

On December 20 Jessup sent two articles, with this comment:

"Well, here's a couple of brief efforts. Use them as you may see fit. They are sufficiently factual to be printable. The Mexican craters are real—I found them myself, and I've seen the airforce negatives.

"The extension of the motive-power theme to include some jolts to religion are rather obvious. This space race COULD be our GOD. They COULD have left the Earth millennia ago. Our book will hint at how Sun-worship may be connected with the space denizens.

"I read your report regarding Albert K. Bender with great interest. Looks like SOMETHING did happen. He probably did stumble onto the truth. I will be glad of any additional information you may uncover.

"In my humble opinion, you are absolutely correct in your thought that the power source is the key to the whole UFO deal. I am convinced of it from my own introspection and reading. I would like to talk to you about."

The above paragraph refers to some ideas I had expressed to Jessup. At that time I thought it possible that the UFO mystery was being "covered up" because of a possible cheap power source which might be revealed if too much became known about the saucers. I had also remarked that a good reason for the saucers' not contacting us might be the possibility that they did not want to reveal their power source to us abruptly in that it would disrupt our economic system).

Following are the two articles submitted to me by Jessup for publication:

• • •

UFO and The Moon
by M. K. Jessup

Astronomers have seen the UFO in space.

The sightings were documented more than 80 years ago. Documented, and measurements made. By triangulation their habitat has been disclosed, and their parent ships identified. Something is known of their size and nature.

They are a part of the Earth-Moon system. Beware of the smokescreen belched forth by Army Ordnance and Dr. Tombaugh who SAY they are looking for small satellites circling the Earth. There is a place where they can look and with likely success—and, they are NOT satellites. Strangely enough, these "things" are just about the right size to fit into a nice big cradle, or crater, such as the one on the Arizona Plateau, and which would just be visible to an Astronomer on the Moon if he possessed a modest-sized telescope.

The Moon has come into the headlines recently in a big way. New cracks have appeared. Craters have disappeared. Craters have appeared. Craters have changed into diffuse, nebulous, brilliant white spots, not focusable in large telescopes which show neighboring surface features with splendid clarity. Cracks, called "rills" for generations, come and go. Mists form within large craters and walled plains.

Lights are seen moving in the dark parts of the Moon. Sometimes an entire large crater, with its central mountain, is lighted with a peculiar and ominous glow.

Walls, or cable-like structures, have appeared ACROSS craters—reported by Flamarrion in the 19th century (See *L' Astronomie*) and by contemporary selonographers in recent news releases. See CRIFO for an object, about the size of a small crater-hollow, leaving the Moon. Dark greenish and brownish shades form within craters and progress with the moving Sun.

In Mexico there is a group of ten craters similar to the Arizona Crater and of just the same size and appearance as the small craters on the Moon. These are recorded on aerial films hoarded by the Airforce, and restricted. They are "classified" and YOU cannot obtain prints of them. Does Ordnance connect these with the "Satellites" which they wish you to believe that they and Tombaugh are looking for? Who knows?

When a lunar crater appears, has it just been evacuated by a resting craft—half a mile or two miles in diameter?

When a crater disappears, and astronomers with powerful telescopes confirm that it is replaced with some sort of DOME, did something settle into that spot for rest or repairs? When it is replaced by a smoke-like nebulosity of changing shape and size, which CASTS NO SHADOW, is something concealing an activity under a cloud from five to eleven miles across?

The Library Research Group has been quietly digging these facts out of scientific literature, old and new. The mass of data is appallingly large. Its coordination is a huge task. Its explanation is slowly becoming more obvious. The Library Research Group is publishing its findings and conclusions in some books about the Scientific Case for UFO.

Conclusions are that the Moon is something else than a dead and useless world. The Earth and Moon form a Binary-planet: a system. There is more in this system than has previously been admitted, even though it has occasionally met the eye. The new books will tell you something about this startling situation. By pure deduction we may be able to say what Bender is prevented from saying.

Gray Barker's Notes

Jessup's reference to Albert K. Bender was made, of course, before Bender told his story in *Flying Saucers and the Three Men*. It is interesting to note that Bender's visitors told him that they lived underground on their home planet, and used craters for entrance and exit. Before Bender "talked" he sent me a drawing for use as a cover for *The Saucerian* (in 1953) illustrating the

The cover of an early issue of *The Saucerian* designed by Albert K. Bender. Now, after nine years have passed, the author reveals the meaning of his drawing.

idea, though at the time I did not know what it was supposed to represent. Bender's drawing still looks suspiciously like a scene on the Moon, and we still wonder if Bender might have known something about the Moon which he later "covered up" in his book. Bender's cover drawing is reproduced, in reduced size, on the previous page.

Jessup, in 1956, wrote me that he had an opportunity to do first-hand research on the Mexican craters:

"Of course, you know of my interests in Mexico, and they have suddenly and unexpectedly come to life: (1) Some commercial interests are probably taking me to Mexico on a preliminary survey for minerals under the meteor craters; and (2) it seems very likely that the government may finance a full-scale expedition through the sponsorship of the University of Michigan.

"On the first I would leave, probably about December 10th, for a five week trip. On the second, it might materialize about April first and last for at least five months. It is alright to mention these things in publication, but do not YET mention the government or the U of M, as no contracts have been signed. To mention them might kill the thing entirely. I may be able to send news items from Mexico."

Something happened to the expeditions, and they never came about. In a subsequent letter Jessup said that the University had backed down because a UFO researcher was involved. Jessup never did reveal the identity of the commercial interests who apparently were interested in financing him.

Some people have suggested that the falling through of these plans was a link in the chain of disappointments which led to suicide. It is indeed true a great deal of the author's hoped-for success never materialized. His second book. The UFO Annual, and The Expanding Case for the UFO did not go well. THE UFO and the Bible, though a popular book among saucer researchers, did not sell well, possibly because of its short length. Incidentally Jessup told me he submitted it to his publisher as a part of his manuscript for The Expanding Case for the UFO and that this particular section was rejected and returned to him for possible expansion into a separate book. This Jessup

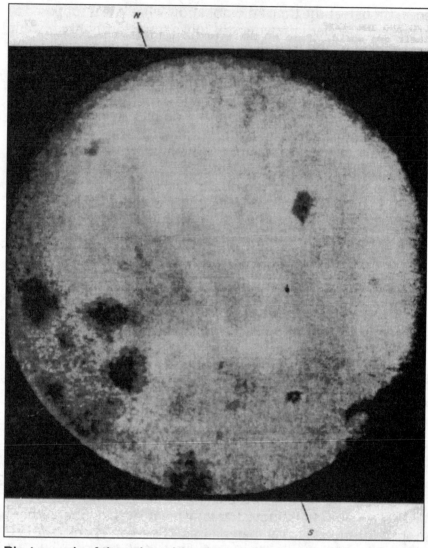

Photograph of the other side of the moon, obtained by the automatic interplanetary station.

did. The book is unfortunately out of print.

To quote from a letter from Jessup, "The *Annual* did not sell very well, and it could not be expected to do so at $4.95. The price is entirely too high. I had expected a cheap, telephone-book style of printing and binding to sell at two or three dollars, but Citadel thought otherwise."

Jessup did not complete his final drafts for his books. This work was done by his literary agent. In the case of *UFO Annual,* his agent simply took files of clippings from Jessup and organized them into book form. This is how an unfortunate portion, involving three strange men allegedly seen in the Pentagon, got into the book. It happened to be a short story from a magazine, which happened to be among the clippings, and the agent included it as if it were fact. Many of Jessup's critics pointed at this, using it as a means of discrediting Jessup's work—though it certainly was not the author's fault.

• • •

Motive Power of the UFO
by M.K. Jessup

The preparation of my book describing the scientific case for the UFO required a tremendous amount of reading and introspection. The case for the UFO is scientifically sound, although still tenuous. Any speculation whatsoever about UFO's must be predicated on whether, in honest fact, the UFO does exist and a modicum of observations are valid as reported. In the present state of "saucer" affairs we cannot but accept their reality.

Once this premise is accepted, a great many conclusions become practically unavoidable. Such elements include the speeds and accelerations observed; the apparent existence of solid but invisible (to the eye) objects in the atmosphere; the ability of large objects to move through the air without overhearing and without seeming to be distorted on their leading edge by air resistance. There are others, of course.

Probably the most basic consideration of all from the viewpoint of science and engineering is the question of motive power. Jets have been suggested, as have rockets. They have to be rejected forthwith because of the inability of carrying fuel and material for reactional ejection. Magnetic drives have been almost universally postulated, so let us consider them for a moment:

The Earth DOES have a very intense magnetic field but it is restricted to the immediate neighborhood of the planet, and is variable and whimsical in its nature and erratically influenced by sun spot activity. Only magnetic and para-magnetic materials can react to the magnetic field, or at best another magnetic field set up by induction. To obtain a space drive from such a mechanism, the thrust must be picked up by the magnet or coil which is reacting with the magnetic field and mechanically transmitting to the craft, and, through the structure of the craft, to the people, animals, beings or entities enclosed in the craft and operating it.

Thus all of the terrific and unbelievable accelerations which have been repeatedly observed must be externally applied to such beings, primate or not, as may be operating the "saucers." The fact that primate beings cannot withstand external pressure and stresses of such magnitude has been used by the scientifically elite as a means of ridiculing the whole idea of the UFO. Granting the reality of the UFO, these observed facts do not negate the UFO, but merely demonstrate the impossibility of externally applied accelerations, due to any cause including jets, rockets or magnetic drives. If neither the structure of the craft nor the sinew of its pilot can withstand such stress—then actual observation demands another power source.

Science to the contrary notwithstanding, there is such a source. It is reaction to the gravitational field, which is universal, and, as compared to the magnetic field, it is relatively uniform and unfluctuating. Wiggle reaction to a magnetic field can be had only from magnetic and metallic materials, reaction to a gravitational field can be had directly from ALL materials having mass. Thus gravitational thrust can be applied to ALL the molecules of any primate being or UFO structure simultaneously and so eliminate external pressure. No calculable amount of acceleration would then be felt by any being subjected to such a force, which would act uniformly through the interior of his body. Not only would there be no harmful results: there would not be ANY sensation of acceleration whatsoever either to the craft or to its operators.

The UFO is propelled by a "cheap" source of power, therefore: a reaction with the gravitational field, comparable to the reactions of the sails of an old fashioned sailing ship with the wind. It is high time we stopped spending the taxpayer's money for impractical rocket development, and invest in basic research to uncover the secret of gravitational drive which was known even to ante-deluvian civilizations.

Gray Barker's Notes

From the beginning of his research, Jessup evidently felt that the saucers were propelled by some sort of "anti-gravity" application. This interest may have been the reason Jessup seemed to be greatly intrigued by the Allende Letters and the Varo Edition of his book, since they suggested some radical new invention involving Einstein's Unified Field theory. It has long been felt by some top UFO researchers that the Government has long sponsored secret development projects which were designed to discover a principle which could control the force of gravity.

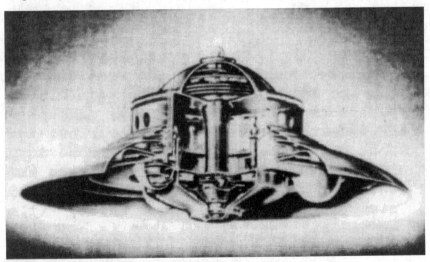

Above: Leonard G. Cramp, in his book, *Space, Gravity and the Flying Saucer* (now out of print), envisioned flying saucers as operating on an anti-gravity principle, and presented this impression of an Adamski-type saucer in cross-section.

Since no workable theory has evidently been developed to date, it is probably a good thing that the government did pursue the development of rockets instead of throwing all its energy behind developing an anti-gravity application which might not have been forthcoming by now. There is no doubt that had our rocket program been pursued as it should have been, we would by now be far ahead of the Soviets in the space race.

The editor has long felt that the development of an anti-gravity application would be the biggest scientific breakthrough since the discovery of atomic power—and probably a much more important one! In fact a monopoly of such a discovery by one country could give it control of the earth!

Department of the Navy at the time the Philadelphia Experiment took place.

Chapter Two
The Case for the UFO

To get to the juncture where the Philadelphia Experiment comes to play a major role in Dr. Morris K. Jessup's life, it is necessary to backtrack somewhat in time. Author of such serious works as *UFOs in the Bible* and *The UFO Annual*, Jessup was highly respected by the public who took his books to heart (though they were never truly best-selling works), as well as by members of the UFO community, who thought him a serious contributor to the body of literature (much of which is otherwise misleading) on the subject.

One of the major parts of the Philadelphia Experiment has to do with a strange, annotated paperback copy of Jessup's *The Case for the UFO*, and the subsequent republication of an annotated copy, allegedly by the military, in a large, offset form.

Once again, Gray Barker was "in" on the early developments directly related to what has become known as the "Varo Edition" of *The Case for the UFO*, so we might be better off allowing him to lay down this remarkable story on our behalf:

• • •

The Strange Annotated Book

One of the major parts of the Jessup mystery is a strange, annotated paperback copy of *The Case for the UFO*, and the subsequent re-publication of the annotated copy, allegedly by the military, in large, mimeographed form.

The paperback copy was marked throughout, with under-

24

linings and notations, evidently by three different persons, for three distinct colors of ink—blue, blue-violet, and blue-green—were used.

The notations were most strange, for they implied intimate knowledge of saucers, their means of propulsion, their origin, background, history, and habits of the beings occupying them.

Nobody seems to come up with the exact proof of the happenings, but since the book allegedly involved the military, that is somewhat understandable. Please bear in mind that in reporting on these incidents, we are reporting mainly what others have told us and published on the subject, and have had no way of thoroughly checking out the information.

According to Riley Crabb, the annotated copy was addressed to Admiral N. Furth, Chief, Office of Naval Research, Washington 25, D. C., and was mailed in a manila envelope postmarked Seminole, Texas, 1955. In July or August of that year the book appeared in the incoming correspondence of Major Darrell L. Ritter, U.S.M.C., Aeronautical Project Office in ONR. When Captain Sidney Sherby reported aboard at ONR he obtained the book from Major Ritter. Captain Sherby and Commander George W. Hoover, Special Projects Officer, ONR, indicated interest in some of the notations the book contained.

I first learned of the annotated copy when I was talking to Mrs. Walton Colcord John, director of the Little Listening Post, a UFO and New Age Publication in Washington. Speaking over the telephone, Mrs. John told me of a strange rumor going around, to the effect that somebody had sent a marked-up copy to Washington, and that the government had gone to the expense of mimeographing the entire book, so that all the underlinings and notations could be added to the original text. This was being circulated rather widely, she told me, through military channels.

She had not, of course, seen a copy of it, and didn't know too much about it, but somehow she seemed to connect it with an alleged Naval experiment wherein a ship had completely disappeared from sight. I couldn't make too much out of all this until later I also heard about the strange Allende Letters, which told of such an experiment in a most horrifying way.

The publication of the mimeographed edition is established, but I have been unable to confirm whether or not it was actually paid for by the government. It is established that the Varo Manufacturing Company, of Garland, Texas, actually produced the mimeographed edition.

I have been unable to find out much about this company, except that it has been said that it engaged in "secret government work."

Apparently Mr. Crabb in some way came into possession of a copy of the special edition, for in his special publication he reproduces the Preface, as closely as possible to the original Varo Edition (we also reproduce this in later pages).

To enable you to better understand our reprint of Mr. Crabb's reproduction, let us try to explain the material in somewhat more detail.

Since three different people evidently made the notations, in different colors of ink, Mr. Crabb refers to them as "Mr. A," "Mr. B," and "Jemi." It was assumed that the third person was "Jemi" because of the direct use of that name in salutations and references by Mr. A and Mr. B throughout the book.

Mr. Crabb believes that it is possible that two of the persons are twins, since there are two references to this word, appearing on pages six and 81 of the original. "The assumption that Mr. A is one of the twins may be correct. On page 81, Mr. A has written and then marked through, '....and I Do Not know How this came to Pass, Jemi.' Then he has written, 'I remember My twin...' On page six he writes in an apparent answer to Mr. B, 'No, My twin....' We cannot be sure of the other twin."

"It is probable," Mr. Crabb continues, "that these men are Gypsies. In the closing pages of the book Mr. B says, '....only a Gypsy will tell another of that catastrophe. And we are a discredited people, ages ago. Hah! Yet, man wonders where "we" come from...' On page 130 Mr. A says, '....ours is a way of life, time proven & happy. We have nothing, own nothing except our music & philosophy & are happy.' On page 76 Mr. B says, 'Show this to a Brother Gypsy....' On page 158 the reference to the word 'we' by Mr. A could refer to the 'discredited people.' Charles G. Leland in his book, '*English Gypsies and Their Lan-*

guage, states that the Gypsies call each other brother and sister, and are not in the habit of admitting to their fellowship people of a different blood and with whom they have no sympathy. This could explain the usage of the term in the closing notes, 'My Dear Brothers,' and perhaps the repeated reference to 'vain humankind'."

The paperback copy of *The Case for the UFO* apparently passed through the hands of these men several times. This conclusion Crabb draws from the fact that there are discussions between two or all three of the men, questions, answers, and places where parts of a note have been marked through, underlined, or added to by one or both of the other men. Some have been deleted by marking through.

I have not seen a copy of the complete, annotated book. Correspondence with Crabb, with whom I discussed a possible reprint of the entire Varo Edition, discouraged me, advising me that the notations and underlinings, in themselves, mean very little, and are "little more than 'teasers'."

In his correspondence with me of September 24, 1962, Crabb clears up the mystery of how he happened to obtain a copy of the original Varo edition. It was the copy that the Navy originally gave to Jessup, and apparently was given to Crabb by Jessup.

This copy, however, rather mysteriously disappeared in April, 1960, when Crabb mailed it to himself from Washington, and apparently he no longer possesses any copy at all.

In elaborating further about the original Varo Edition, Crabb writes, "It may be that CDR Hoover, or some other open-minded officer in the Office of Navy Research asked Varo to print the notes and the book; on the other hand, maybe Bob Jordan or some other official at Varo, in Washington at the time, sniffed a possible research and development project, and volunteered to do it. Anyhow, I understand that 25 copies were reproduced on standard letter paper, 8½ x 11, probably on Varo's own little litho press, and plastic bound, pretty close to 200 pages. Michael Ann Dunn, the stenographer who did the editing, explains why in the introduction. She's married now, living in Dallas, and won't answer her phone. Garland (where Varo is located) is a Dallas suburb. I suppose Varo and/or the Navy judiciously handed out a few copies to those capable of picking up a hot lead on the anti-gravity research trail. From their comment, Allende and his gypsy friends were not educated, not technicians, and did not give any illustrations or mathematical formulae which would help build usable hardware.

"Varo, by the way, is a small manufacturing firm in electronics and up to its neck in space age business. Apparently it has succeeded in developing some kind of a death ray gadget, judging from a guarded press release of last fall when a group of Congressmen visited there for a demonstration. I think it extremely interesting that certain Naval officers and Varo officials took the Allende notes far more seriously at first reading than did Jessup himself! My first reaction to them was one of skepticism, but now I believe them. So does one of our most material minded, hardest headed electronic engineer associates in Los Angeles."

• • •

Indeed, why all the fuss and bother over a strange marked up book that even Jessup himself thought was "crackpot"? It is not so much the contents of the notations but the importance that evidently was attached to them.

I had heard about the matter but figured there was very little to it, until I happened to run into Ivan Sanderson, noted naturalist and UFO expert, in New York.

I knew that Ivan had been a close friend of Jessup and felt that by talking to him on this subject I might get some clue as to the reason for the suicide—if indeed it had been that. I found that Ivan would not discuss this particular matter, but that he was willing to give me a great deal of information about the Varo Edition.

Since I am speaking of our conversation from memory, I may not have all the details as they were given to me, but will do the best I can to report on it.

I wondered why Jessup had never publicized the matter.

"There was probably good reason for that," Ivan told me. "He had been called up to Annapolis, where he was dumbfounded when Naval Intelligence showed him a large mimeo-graphed book, consisting of the text of his book, along with underlinings and notes. This was particularly puzzling to him, in that, to him, as a UFO researcher, the various scribbled remarks and underlinings sounded utterly ridiculous.

"Why had they gone to so much trouble, and evidently spent a lot of money, too, on this deal? That was what ran through Morris' mind. I suppose he never did find out."

● ● ●

It would be, of course, impossible for us to reproduce the entire Varo Edition, even were we in the possession of the complete text. We will, however, reproduce the Preface, which is available, in a form as close to the Varo edition as is possible.

As to the complete text, we quote Crabb's explanation:

"The notes (added by the Gypsies) refer to two types of people living in space. Specifically the 'stasis neutral' and undersea are mentioned as habitats. They seem to live in both interchangeably. The building of undersea cities is mentioned. Many different kinds of ships are used as transportation. These two peoples, races or whatever they may be called, are referred to, over and over again. They are called L-M's and S-M's. The L-M's seem to be peaceful; the S-M's are not. It seems that the annotations are inclined toward the L-M's as they speak more kindly of them than the S-M's.

"Terms such as: mothership, home-ship, Great Ark, great bombardment, great return, great war, little-men, force-fields, deep freezes, undersea building, measure markers, scout ships, magnetic and gravity fields, sheets of diamond, cosmic rays, force cutters, undersea explorers, inlay work, clear-talk, tele-pathing, burning 'coat', nodes, vortice, magnetic 'net,' and many others are used quite naturally by these men. They explain how, why, and what happens to people, ships, and planes that have disappeared. They explain the origin of odd storms and clouds, objects falling from the sky, strange marks and footprints, and other things which we have not solved.

"These men seem to feel that it is too late for man to obtain space flight. They feel that mankind could not cope with 'those mind wrecking conditions that space and sea contain' for mankind is too egotistical, values too much the material, wars over mere parcels of this planet, is too filled with jealousy, and lacks true brotherhood.

"It may be that the underscore in the book was in the form of a code or that if read separately that it would have a meaning of its own. Superficial examination has failed to disclose such a code. The underscored text usually refers to the notes by the same man."

Notes on the Following Reproduction

In reproducing the Preface from the Varo Edition of *The Case for the UFO,* we have tried to copy it as closely as possible.

Some explanation is needed to understand the notes in relationship to the text, as published in this form.

The distinction between the text of the original book and the handwritten additions made to it is made by the use of indentations of nine spaces, whereas paragraphs of Jessup's original text are indented only five spaces. In other words, nine-space indentations indicate the annotations made in handwriting by Mr. A, Mr. B, or Jemi to the original.

The placement of the notes indicates the paragraph to which they refer, or to their precise position in the book.

The page numbers of the original book are denoted in parentheses. The matter on the page numbered follows the number. The page numbers of this edition appear at the bottom of each page.

It has been necessary to disregard the italics of the original.

The reprint of this Preface is not intended to offer a great deal of information, but is presented, to the researcher, as a sampling of the Varo Edition.

Preface (Varo Edition)

The subject of UFO's in its present stage is like astronomy in that it is a purely observational "science," not an experimental one; necessarily, therefore, it must be based on observation and not on experiment. Observation, in this case, consists of everything which can be found to have bearing on the subject.

There are thousands of references to it in ancient literature, but the authors did not know that their references had any bearing, for the subject did not then exist. The writers were recording such things as met their senses solely through an honest effort to report inexplicable observational data. (B)

Hoping, in those days, that something would "come of (Mr.B) it" Nowadays, Science is afraid that "Something Will Come of it." It will, too. In 1956 or 57 the Air force *Will have* Ships LIKE these in appearance & Will "feel" safe to announce that Human eyes Have seen Saucers from outer Space But to Not be Worried because "We too have these Ships" Oh! Brother What a farce! ours will be JET propelled not *M.* propelled.

Some of my contemporaries have attempted to prove that all of these phenomena are, in some way or other, illusory, and that in any case they do not involve flight, wingless or otherwise, mechanical propulsion or intelligent direction.

I consider their negative unproven because *there is an overwhelming mass of authentic evidence* which can be cited as: (1) direct observation, (2) indirect observation, and (3) supporting evidence or indication. (B)

There is one sphere of indirect evidence in the form of events of mysterious nature which have never been explained. These things would be easy to explain were we to admit the limitations of our own knowledge, and the possibility of "intelligence" elsewhere in the universe operating space ships—and quite possibly more than one kind of "intelligence" and more than one kind of space ship.

(vi)

This world is full of unexplained oddities. The legends of Atlantis and Mu have been favorite targets of the scoffers. "They" *say* there are no ghosts, no spirits, nothing falls from the sky but iron and stone meteorites. But for centuries the earth was believed to be flat, there was no America, no heliocentric system of earth and planets, no fossil dinosaurs; *yet we now know these beliefs to have been wrong.* (B)

Reliable people have been *seeing* the phenomena known as

31

flying saucers *for a thousand years and more*. There are good reports as (B) far back as 1500 B.C. and before. *Thousands of people have seen some kind of navigable contraptions in the sky, and some have sworn it under oath.* (B)

iv

In a day When oaths were just as good as Money-in (Mr. B) Hand for if incorrect your neck suffered "The Miracle" (1) from the Church as a knife from the outraged who *took* your oath.

I cannot agree with any astronomer who insists that all of these things are mirages, planets, clouds or illusions. The majority of the people are articulate enough to tell their stories, and sincere enough to make depositions before notaries public. Even scientists concede that these folk saw something.

I see nothing particularly odd in strange descriptions of phenomena the like of which has no earthly counterpart or for which we have no frame of reference. (B)

If he does not, then he KNOWS the L-M's. (Mr. B)

This work is a serious attempt to bring order out of chaos, an attempt to pull all of the facets of this controversy into a basic stratum *upon which to make an intelligent evaluation of the subject.* (B)

M. K. Jessup

Washington, D. C. January 13, 1955

If he does succeed in such evaluation Nobody (Mr. B) cares enough to bother believing him for that would require the effort of Courage & The Gaiyar are such cowards & conformists. Even if believed, Nobody would *dare* say so for that would require action & They dare not act in BEHALF OF A BELIEF THAT INTERFERES WITH USUAL LIVING.

(1) Undecipherable: could be Nracle or Nrack.

Some hard core debunkers of the Philadelphia Experiment have long insisted that Carlos Allende (also known as Carl M. Allen) never existed. Documents show he was an able-bodied seaman until his death.

Chapter Three
Who Was
Carlos Allende?

One of the strangest men to be found on the face of the planet calls himself Carlos Miguel Allende. He may still be "alive" today—though it is thought that he passed away a number of years ago.

Allende remains an enigma to those few he knew quite well.

To those who did not have a personal insight into his manner and his reason for being, he might have been thought of as a real mad man, someone who should be locked away in a mental institution.

For Allende claimed to have been a survivor of the Philadelphia Experiment—or at least in a number of letters to Jessup he suggested he might have been.

The letters are somewhat difficult to follow—this I would be the first to admit. Yet once you come to grips with Allende's grammar and writing style, you realize that there is a very tormented individual beneath the writing—someone who lives in stark terror day or night. He is the type of person who is constantly looking over his shoulder, looking for someone—anyone—who might be making his life a living hell.

It all started on January 13, 1956—many years ago now—when Dr. Jessup received a letter from Carlos Miguel Allende, who signed his name simply as Carl M. Allen. The letter was sent to Jessup in an envelope bearing the address Turner Hotel,

A rare photo of the mysterious Carlos Miguel Allende.

Gainesville, Texas. It had no return address, but was evidently postmarked from somewhere in the state of Pennsylvania.

Due to the uniqueness of Allende's spelling and grammar, it became almost immediately evident to Jessup that Allende was possibly one of those who had worked on the annotation of the Varo Edition of his book, and was very likely the same individual who had originally mailed the volume to the Navy (why would they have paid any attention to someone whose name they did not recognize as having been in the service and perhaps affiliated with the Philadelphia Experiment?).

In the letter, we are given the first clues about the Philadelphia Experiment and what actually happened back in 1943. Allende let the cat out of the bag for better or for worse, and his story as to what happened has become part of American culture since that time.

But let us see what Allende had to say for himself in these remarkable "tell all" letters addressed to Dr. Morris K. Jessup. Please note that I have not changed Allende's peculiar punctuation and syntax, so you can get a "feel" for his odd writing style and his unusual brand of evidence.

• • •

Carlos Miguel Allende
R.D. #1, Box 223
New Kensington, Penn.

My Dear Dr. Jessup,
Your invocation to the Public that they move en Masse upon their Representatives and have thusly enough Pressure placed at the right & sufficient Number of Places where from a Law demanding Research into Dr. Albert Einsteins Unified Field Theory May be enacted (1925–27) *is Not* at all Necessary. It May Interest you to know that The Good Doctor Was Not so Much influenced in his retraction of that Work, by Mathematics, as he most assuredly was by Humantics.

His Later computations, done strictly for his own edification & amusement, upon cycles of Human Civilization & Progress compared to the Growth of Mans General over-all Character Was enough to Horrify Him. Thus, We are *"told"* today that that Theory was "Incomplete."

Dr. B. Russell asserts privately that It is complete. He also says that Man is Not Ready for it & Shan't be until after W.W. III. Nevertheless, "Results" of My friend Dr. Franklin Reno, *Were used.* These Were a complete Recheck of That Theory, With a View to any & Every Possible quick use of it, if leasable in a Very short time. There Were good Results, as far as a Group Math Re-Check AND as far as a good Physical "Result," to Boot. YET, THE NAVY FEARS TO USE THIS RESULT. The Result was & stands today as Proof that The Unified Field Theory to a certain extent is correct. Beyond that certain extent No Person in his right senses, or having any senses at all, Will evermore *dare* to go. I am sorry that I have Mislead You in My Previous Missive. True, enough, such a form of Levitation has been accomplished as described. It is also a Very commonly observed reaction of certain Metals to Certain Fields surrounding a current. This field being used for that purpose. Had Farraday concerned himself about the Mag. field surrounding an Electric Current, We today Would NOT exist *or if* We did exist, our present Geo-political situation would have the very time-bomish, ticking off towards Destruction, atmosphere that Now exists. Alright, Alright! The "result" was complete invisibility of a ship, Destroyer type, *and all* of its crew, While at Sea. (Oct. 1943) The Field Was effective in an oblate spheroidal shape, extending one hundred yards (More or Less, due to Lunar position & Latitude) *out* from each beam of the ship. Any Person Within that sphere became vague in form BUT He too observed those Persons aboard *that* ship as though they too were of the same state, yet were walking upon nothing. Any person without that sphere could see Nothing save the clearly *Defined shape of the Ships Hull in the Water,* PROVIDING of course, that that person was just close enough to see, yet, just barely outside of that field. Why tell you Now? Very Simple; If You choose to go Mad, then you would reveal this information. Half of the officers & the crew of that Ship are at present, Mad as Hatters. A few, are even Yet, confined to certain areas where they May receive trained Scientific aid when they, either, "Go Blank" or "Go Blank" & Get Stuck." Going-Blank IE an after effect of the Man having been within the field too Much, IS Not at all an unpleasant experience to Healthily Curious Sailors. However it is when also, they "Get Stuck" that they call it "HELL" INCORPORATED" The Man thusly stricken can Not Move of his own volition unless two or More of those who are within the field go & touch him, quickly, else he "Freezes".

If a Man Freezes, His position Must be Marked out carefully and then the Field is cut-off. Everyone but that "Frozen" Man is able to Move; to appreciate *apparent* Solidity again. Then, the Newest Member of the crew Must approach the Spot, where he will find the "Frozen" Mans face or Bare Skin, that is Not covered by usual uniform Clothing. Sometimes, It takes only an hour or so Sometimes all Night & all Day Long & Worse *It once took 6 months, to get The Man "Unfrozen". This "Deep Freeze" was not psychological.* It is the Result of a Hyper-Field that is set up, *within* the field of the Body, While The "Scorch" Field is turned on & this at Length *or* upon a Old Hand.

A Highly complicated Piece of Equipment Had to be constructed in order to Unfreeze those who became "True Froze" (1) or "Deep Freeze" subjects. *Usually a "Deep Freeze" Man goes Mad, Stark Raving, Gibbering, Running Mad,* if His "freeze" is far More than a Day in our time.

I speak of TIME for DEEP "Frozen Men" are Not aware of Time as We know it. They are Like Semi-comatose person, who Live, breathe, Look & feel but still are unaware of So Utterly Many things as to constitute a "Nether World" to them. A Man in an ordinary common Freeze *is* aware of Time, Sometimes *acutely* so. Yet They are Never aware of Time precisely as you or I are

(1) Could be "Free Freeze" aware of it. The First "Deep Freeze" as I said took 6 months to Rectify. It also took over 5 Million Dollars worth of Electronic equipment & a Special Ship Berth. If around or Near the Philadelphia Navy Yard you see a group of Sailors in the act of Putting their Hands *upon* a fellow *or* upon "thin air," observe the Digits & appendages of the Stricken Man. If they seem to Waver, as tho within a Heat-Mirage, *go quickly* & Put YOUR Hands upon Him, *For that Man is The Very Most Desperate of Men in The World. Not one of those Men ever want at all to become again invisible.* I do Not think that Much More Need be said as to Why Man is Not Ready for Force-Field Work. Eh?

You Will Hear phrases from these Men such as "Caught in the Flow (or the Push) or "Stuck in the Green" or "Stuck in Molasses" or "I was "going" FAST", These Refer to Some of the Decade-Later after effects of Force-Field Work. "Caught in the Flow" Describes exactly the "Stuck in Molasses" sensation of a Man going into a "Deep Freeze" or Plain Freeze" either of the two. "Caught in the Push" can either refer to That Which a

Man feels Briefly WHEN he is either about to inadvertently "Go-Blank" IE Become Invisible" or about to "Get Stuck" in a "Deep Freeze" or "Plain Freeze."

There are only a very few of the original Experimental D-E's Crew Left by Now, Sir. Most went insane, one just walked "through" His quarters Wall in sight of His Wife & Child & 2 other crew Members (WAS NEVER SEEN AGAIN), two "Went into "The Flame," I.E. They "Froze" & caught fire, while carrying common Small-Boat Compasses, one Man carried the compass & Caught fire, the other came for the "Laying on of Hands" as he was nearest but he too, took fire. THEY BURNED FOR 18 DAYS. The faith in "Hand Laying" Died When this Happened & Mens Minds Went by the scores. *The experiment Was a Complete Success. The Men Were Complete Failures.*

Check Philadelphia Papers for a tiny one Paragraph (upper Half of sheet, inside the paper Near the rear 3rd of Paper, 1944–46 in Spring or Fall or Winter, NOT Summer.) of an Item describing the Sailors Actions after their initial Voyage. They Raided a Local to the Navy Yard "Gin Mill" or "Beer Joint" & caused such Shock & Paralysis of the Waitresses that Little comprehensible could be gotten from them, save that Paragraph & the Writer of it, Does Not Believe it, & Says, "I only wrote what I heard & them Dames is Daffy. So, all I get is a "Hideit" Bedtime Story."

Check observer ships crew, Matson Lines Liberty ship out of Norfolk (Company MAY Have Ships Log for that Voyage or Coast Guard have it) The S.S. Andrew Furnseth, Chief Mate Mowsely, (Will secure Captains Name Later) (Ships Log Has Crew List on it.) one crew member Richard Price or "Splicey" Price May Remember other Names of Deck Crew Men, (Coast Guard has record of Sailors issued "Papers") Mr. Price Was 18 or 19 then, Oct. 1943, and Lives or Lived at that time in His old Family Home in Roanoke, VA. a small town with a Small Phone book. These Men Were Witnesses, The Men of this crew, "Connally of New England, (Boston?), May have Witnessed but I doubt it. (Spelling May be incorrect) DID Witness this. I ask you to Do this bit of Research simply that you May Choke on your own Tongue when you Remember what you have "appealed be

Made Law"

Very Disrespectfully Yours,
Carl M. Allen

P.S. Will Help More if you see Where I can. (Z416175)

Days Later
Notes in addition to and pertaining to Missive.
(Contact Rear Admiral Ransom Bennett for verifica-
tion of info Herein. Navy Cheif of research. He may
offer you a job, ultimately)

Coldly & analytically speaking, without the Howling that
is in the Letter to you accompanying this, I will say the following in all Fairness to you & to Science. (1) The Navy did Not
know that the men could become invisible WHILE NOT UPON
THE SHIP & UNDER THE FIELDS INFLUENCE. (2) The Navy
Did Not know that *there would be* Men Die from odd effects of
HYPER "Field" within or upon "Field." (3) Further, They even
yet do Not know Why this happened & are not even sure that
the "F" within "F" is the reason, for sure at all. *In Short* The
Atomic bomb didn't kill the experimentors thus the experiments went on-but eventually one or two were accidentally
killed But *the cause* was known as to *Why* they died. Myself, I
"feel" that something pertaining to that Small-boat compass
"triggered" off "The Flames." I have no proof, but Neither Does
the Navy. (4) WORSE & Not Mentioned When one or two of
their Men, Visible-within-the-field-to-all-the-others, *Just Walked
into Nothingness,* AND Nothing Could be felt, of them, either
when the "field" Was turned on OR off, THEY WERE JUST
GONE! *Then,* More Fears Were Amassed. (5) Worse, Yet, When
an apparently Visible & New-Man Just walks seemingly
"through" the Wall of his House, the surrounding area Searched
by all Men & thoroughly scrutinized by & with & under an
Installed Portable Field developer *AND* NOTHING EVER found
of him. *So Many Many Fears were by then in effect that the Sum
total of them all could Not ever again be faced by ANY of those Men
or by the Men Working at & upon the Experiments.*

40

I wish to Mention that Somehow, also, The Experimental Ship Disappeared from its Philadelphia Dock and only a Very few Minutes Later appeared at its other Dock in the Norfolk, Newport News, Portsmouth area. This was distinctly AND clearly Identified as being that place BUT the ship then, *again* Disappeared And Went Back to its Philadelphia Dock in only a Very few Minutes or Less. This was also noted in the newspapers But I forget what paper I read it in or When It happened. Probably Late in the experiments, May have been in 1956 *after* Experiments were discontinued, I can Not Say for Sure.

To the Navy this Whole thing was So Impractical due to its Morale Blasting effects Which were so much so that efficient operation of the Ship was Drastically hindered and then after this occurrence It was shown that even the Mere operation of a ship could Not be counted upon at all. In short, Ignorance of this thing bred Such Terrors of it that, on the Level of attempted operations, with what knowledge was then available It was deemed as impossible, Impracticable and Too Horrible.

I believe that had YOU *then* been Working upon & With the team that was Working upon this project With yourself knowing what You *NOW* know, *that* "The Flames" Would Not have been *so unexpected,* or Such a Terrifying Mystery. Also, More than Likely, I must say in All fairness, None of these other occurrences could have happened without some knowledge of their possibility of occurring. In fact, They May have been prevented by a far More Cautious Program AND by a Much More Cautiously careful Selection of Personnel for Ships officers & Crew. Such Was Not the case. The Navy used whatever *Human Material* was at hand, Without Much, *if any,* thought as to character & Personality of that Material. If care, Great Care is taken in selection of Ship, and officers and crew AND If Careful Indoctrination is taken *along* with Careful watch over articles of apparel such as rings & Watches & Identification bracelets & belt buckles, Plus AND ESPECIALLY the effect of Hob-Nailed shoes or Cleated-shoes U.S. Navy issues shoes, I feel that some progress toward dissipating the fear-filled ignorance surrounding this project Will be Most surely & certainly accomplished. The Records of the U.S. Maritime *Service,* HOUSE Norfolk Va.

(for Graduated Seamen of their Schools) Will reveal Who was assigned to S.S. *Andrew Furnseth* for Month of either Late Sept. or Oct. of 1943. I remember positively of one other observer who stood beside Me When tests were going on. He was from New England, Brown Blond Curly Hair, blue eyes, Don't remember Name. I leave it up *to you* to Decide if further Work shall be put into this or Not, and Write this in Hopes there Will be.

Very Sincerely, Carl M. Allen

• • •

The second letter received by Jessup from Carlos Allende:

Carl M. Allen
RFD #1 Box 223
New Kensington, Pa.

Dear Mr. Jessup:

Having just recently gotten home from my long travels around the country I find that you had dropped me a card. You ask that I write you "at once" and So after taking everything into consideration, I have decided to do so. You ask me for what is tantamount to positive proof of something that only the duplication of those devices that produced "This phenomenon" could ever give you. at least, were I of scientific bent, I presume that, were I of Such a Curiosity about something, the which has been produced from a theory that was discarded (1927) as incomplete, I am sure that I would be of such a dubiousness towards that I would Have to be *shown* those devices that produced such a curious interaction of Forces & Fields, in operation & their product Mr. Jessup, I could NEVER possibly satisfy such an attitude. The reason being that I could not, Nor ever would the Navy Research Dept. (Then under the present Boss of the Navy, Burke) ever let it be known that any such thing was ever allowed to be done. For you see, It was because of Burkes Curiosity & Willingness & prompting that this experiment was enabled to be carried out. It proved a White-elephant *but* His attitude towards advanced & ultra-advanced types of

42

research is just "THE" THING that put him where he is today. (Or at least, to be sure, It carries a great weight). Were the stench of such an Experiment results EVER to come out, He would be crucified.

However, I have noticed, that through the ages, those who have had this happen to them, once the vulgar passions that caused the reaction have cooled-off AND *further* research OPENLY carried on, *that* these crucified ones achieve something akin to Saint hood. You say that this, "is of the greatest importance". I disagree with you Mr. Jessup, not just whole Heartedly, *but vehemently.* However at the same time, your ideas & your own sort of curiosity is that of mine own sort and besides my disagreement is based upon philosophical Morality and not upon that curiosity which Drives Science so rapidly. I can be of some positive help to you in myself *but* to do so would require a Hypnotist, Sodium Pentathol, a tape recorder & an excellent typist-secretary in order to produce material of *Real* value to you.

As you know one who is hypnotized cannot Lie *and* one who is both hypnotized AND given "Truth serum" as it is colloquially known, COULD NOT POSSIBLY LIE, *AT ALL.* To boot, *My Memory* would be THUS enabled to remember things in such *great detail,* things that my present consciousness cannot recall at all, or only barely and uncertainly that it would be of far greater benefit to use hypnosis. I could thus be enabled to *not only* Recall COMPLETE Names, but also addresses & telephone numbers AND perhaps the *very* important Z numbers of those sailors whom I sailed with them or even came into contact with. I could too, being something of a Dialectician, be able to thusly talk exactly as these witnesses talked and imitate or *illustrate* their Mannerisms & *Habits of thought,* thus your psychologists can figure IN ADVANCE the Sure-fire method of dealing Most Successfully with these. I could NOT do this with someone with whom I had not observed at length & these men, I lived with for about 6 months, so you are bound to get good to excellent results. *The mind does NOT ever forget, Not really; As you know.* Upon this I suggest this way of doing this with Myself but further, the Latter usage of Myself in Mannerism & Thought pattern illustration is suggested in order that the Goal of inducing these Men to *place themselves* at & under your disposal (HYPNOTICALLY OR UNDER TRUTH-SERUM) is a Goal, the Which could Have Far greater impact, due to correlation of Experiences remembered Hypnotically *by Men who have NOT seen or even written to each other, at all, for Nearly or over TEN years.* In this, With such Men as Witnesses, giving irrefutable testimony It is my belief that were, Not the Navy, *but the Air force,* confronted with such evidence (IE Chief of Research) there would be either an uproar or a quiet and determined effort to achieve Metallic & organic invisibility nor did they fail to, unbesoughtedly, achieve transportation of thousands of tons of Metal & Humans at an eyes blink speed. Even though this latter effect of prolonged experimentation was (to them) The thing that caused them to consider the experiment as a failure, I BELIEVE THAT *FURTHER* EXPERIMENTS WOULD NATURALLY HAVE PRODUCED *CONTROLLED* TRANSPORT OF GREAT TONNAGES AT ULTRA-FAST SPEEDS TO A *DESIRED* POINT THE INSTANT IT IS DESIRED through usage of an area covered by: (1) those cargoes and (2) that "Field" that could cause those goods, Ships or Ship parts (MEN WERE TRANSPORTED AS WELL) *to go* to another Point. Accidentally & to the embarrassed perplexity of the Navy THIS HAS ALREADY HAPPENED TO A WHOLE SHIP, CREW & ALL. *I read of this AND* of THE OFF-BASE AWOL ACTIVITIES OF THE crew-Men who were *at the time* invisible *in* a Philadelphia NEWSPAPER. UNDER HARCO-HYPNOSIS I CAN BE ENABLED TO DIVULGE THE NAME, DATE & SECTION & PAGE NUMBER OF THAT Paper & the other one. *Thus* this papers "Morgue" will divulge EVEN MORE POSITIVE PROOF ALREADY PUBLISHED of this experiment. The Name of the REPORTER who skeptically *covered & wrote* of these incidents (OF THE RESTAURANT-BARROOM RAID WHILE INVISIBLE & OF *THE SHIPS* SUDDENLY AWOL) AND WHO INTERVIEWED the Waitresses CAN THIS BE FOUND, thus HIS and the Waitresses testimony can be added to the Records. Once on this track, I believe That you can uncover CONSIDERABLY MORE evidence to sustain this—(what would you call it—SCANDAL or DISCOVERY?) You would Need a Dale

Carnegie to *Maneuver these folks* into doing just as you wish. It would be cheaper than paying everyone of all these witnesses & *Much more Ethical.* The Idea Is, to the Layman type of person, utterly ridiculous. However, can you remember, all by yourself, the Date of a Newspaper in which you saw an interesting item more than 5 years ago? Or recall names of Men, their phone #'s that you saw in 1943–44.

I do hope you will consider this plan. You will Progress as Not possible in any other way. Of course, I realize that you would need a Man Who can cause people to want to have fun to play with Hypnotism, one that can thusly dupe those you need to: #1 come to His Demonstrations & thus call on them to be either or both "Honored" as Helping with the show" & for doing Him a Great favor, &/ or being part of the act for the mite of a small fee He would HAVE to be a Man of such an adroit ingenuity at Manufacturing a *plausible* story on the-instant-the-sizes-up-his-"*personality-to be dealt with* THAT had cost PLENTY. The ability to convince people of an outright Lie as being the absolute truth would be one of his prime prerequisites. (Ahem.) Yes, some such skulduggery would have to be thought well out & done. THE ULTIMATE END WILL BE A TRUTH TOO HUGE, TOO FANTASTIC, TO NOT BE TOLD. A WELL FOUNDED TRUTH, BACKED UP BY UNOBFUSCATIVE PROOF POSITIVE. *I would like to find where is that these Sailors live NOW.* It is known that some few people can somehow tell you a mans name & His Home address UNDER HYPNOSIS EVEN THOUGH *NEVER* HAVING EVER MET OR SEEN THE PERSON. These folks have a very high or just a high PSI factor in their make-up that can be intensified under stress or strain OR that usually *is* intensified under extreme fright. It also can be RE-intensified by Hypnosis, *thus* is like reading from the Encyclopedia Britannica. Even though that Barroom-Restaurant Raid was staged by invisible or partly invisible men, those men *CAN SEE EACH OTHER* THUS NAMES, In the excitement, *were* sure to have been Mentioned, whether last or first Names or Nicknames. A check of the Naval Yards Dispensaries or Hospital or aid stations or prison RECORDS of that particular day that the Barroom-Restaurant occurred May reveal the EXACT NAMES OF PRECISELY WHO

WERE THE MEN, THEIR SERVICE SERIAL NUMBERS & THUS THE INFORMATION ON WHERE THEY ARE *FROM* TO BE SECURED & by adroit "Maneuverings" of those still at Home, THE NAME OF *THE PLACE* where they are at present can be secured.

HOW WOULD YOU LIKE TO ACTUALLY SPEAK TO (or some of *THE MEN*) A MAN WHO WAS ONCE *AN INVISIBLE HUMAN BEING?* (MAY BECOME SO IN FRONT OF YOUR VERY EYES IF HE TURNS-OFF HIS HIP SET) Well, all this fantastically Preposterous sort of rubbish *will be* necessary, Just to do that, the Hypnotist-psychologist & all that. Maybe I suggest something *too* thorough & *too* Methodical for your taste but then, I, as first subject, Don't care to be Hypnotized *at all,* But too, feel that certain pull of curiosity about this thing that, to me, is irresistible. I *want* to crack this thing wide open. My reasons are simply to enable *more work* to be done upon this "Field Theory."

I am a star-gazer Mr. Jessup. I make no bones about this and the fact that I feel that *IF HANDLED PROPERLY, I.E. PRESENTED TO PEOPLE & SCIENCE IN THE PROPER PSYCHOLOGICALLY EFFECTIVE MANNER,* I feel sure that Man will go where He now dreams of being—to the stars via the form of transport that the Navy accidentally stumbled upon (to their embarrassment) when their EXP. SHIP took off & popped-up a minute or so later on several Hundred sea travel-trips miles away at another of its Berths in the Chesapeake Bay area. I read of *this* in another news paper & only by Hypnosis could *any* Man remember *all* the details of which paper, date of occurrence & etc., you see? Eh. Perhaps already the Navy has used this accident of transport to build your UFOs. It is a logical advance from any standpoint. What do *you* think???

VERY RESPECTFULLY
Carl Allen

THE STRANGE CASE

OF DR. M. K. JESSUP

Edited By Gray Barker

ILLUSTRATED

SAUCERIAN BOOKS
CLARKSBURG, W. VA.

Limited circulation publication put out by the late Gray Barker's Saucerian Press is now a hot collector's item.

Chapter Four
Jessup's Death
Was Not a "Suicide"!

No matter what anyone says, I have good reason to *know* that Dr. Jessup did NOT take his own life as we have been led to believe, but that he was a "victim" of "circumstances."

Apparently, from classified documents I have seen, Jessup was on the verge of getting someone in the Navy to cooperate with him. This individual was going to provide all the evidence to prove to the world that the Philadelphia Experiment really did take place. This is the reason Dr. Jessup was SILENCED. If he had lived all of this would be out in the open a long time ago.

Jessup's passing is a sad and tragic matter, but as far as I am concerned, it is an open and shut case of murder involving a cover-up of great magnitude. Gray Barker, once more, had the inside track on Jessup's demise from the start. He has kept all the facts and figures—all the records—to prove that Jessup was involved in foul play:

• • •

The weather was clear, warm, with only a slight breeze coming in off the ocean. There had been a few showers earlier, but again all was clear. It was one of the warm evenings that South Florida is so famous for.

At Matheson Hammock Park, attendant John Goode was making his usual rounds, just before sundown, closing time, which would come at 6:45 on April 20, 1959. Entering the

48

south picnic parking area off Old Cutler Road, he noticed a white Chevy station wagon parked on the side of the lot.

Goode drove on by; then he thought that he would stop and notify the driver of the closing time. As he braked to a stop, something unusual about the car drove him to look more closely at his rear-view mirror. Then, with a spinning of wheels, he turned and sped back, for there was something unusual about the rear window of the wagon.

It was rolled down an inch or two, and a hose protruded from it. As he stopped, his worst fears found confirmation: the hose was attached to the exhaust pipe, and rags were stuffed tight around it and in the opening!

He pulled the door open and coughed from the heavy fumes, then held his breath while he turned off the ignition. Then he turned his attention to the driver.

The man still sat upright, with a backward slump. His eyes stared straight ahead. Good knew he was dead or very near to it. He opened the door on the driver's right, and drove as fast as he could to the Administration Office to summon help.

There his halting, out-of-breath report would open one of the most controversial chapters in the annals of UFOlogy.

● ● ●

We are told over and over that those who knew Jessup even in the slightest realized full well that he did not commit suicide, for he had not been depressed or given signs of turbulence in his personal life. He appeared to be happy, had a job, a family, lots of friends, and was putting a great deal of effort into his UFO studies. His mistake was perhaps linking them with the Philadelphia Experiment, because this is in all likelihood what caused him to be a prime target for silencing.

According to Gray Barker, years passed following Jessup's demise and almost everyone in the UFO field had forgotten about him—that is except for one woman who got in touch with Barker to tell the researcher of her findings:

● ● ●

The phone rang. It was Ann Gizlinger of Miami, Florida,

whom I had never heard of. She was extraordinarily interested in Jessup's death and subjected me to a kind of "third degree" about what all I knew. Finally, I told her, "Look, let me send you two books, you read them, and then I'll try to answer any questions you have." Accordingly, I shipped out the Annotated Edition of *The Case for the UFO,* and *The Strange Case of Dr. M.K. Jessup.*

I had been getting a number of letters on the subject after Charles Berlitz's book, *Without A Trace,* was published. I assumed she, like others, had simply been intrigued by the section about Jessup and wanted more information. Little did I know then about my further involvement with Ann, nor the strange but fascinating reason that the subject had become almost a fixation in her life.

Nor was I prepared for the extraordinary speed of the Postal Service or Ann's speed reading. Five days later, the phone rang and she was talking my ears off again!

"I don't believe Dr. Jessup took his own life!" she stated. "Or if he did, I believe he did it because of some kind of mind control.

"Part of it is a hunch. I don't want to explain right now. Some of it is from your two books, which I have just finished reading. But the most of it comes from my investigation at the Medical Examiner's office."

Jessup's File

During the months that followed, Ann and I kept in regular communication as we compared notes on what I knew and what she was finding out. The big breakthrough came at the Medical Examiner's office, where Ann felt she might meet with rebuff in trying to reopen this old case. But, surprisingly, she found doors eagerly opened for her and the utmost in cooperation by both the staff and Examiner, Joseph H. Davis. Ordinarily, these medical records aren't just available to the public, yet she was allowed complete access to them and to voice copy them onto tape. As it had been more than ten years since Jessup's death, she had feared the information might be stored in inactive files in some inaccessible location. Again, to her surprise, she found the file still in the current section!

"I now know that this file is still open and is being updated," she told me, "because, during my second inspection, I noticed that the information I had given Davis had been added to it."

When I learned that the current Examiner was Dr. Davis, the extraordinary cooperation made sense. For he had held that same post at the time of Jessup's death, and exhibited more than a perfunctory interested in the case at the time. In fact, he had written to me for more information I had published, asking me if I knew of any instances of the use of hallucinogenic drugs as techniques in UFO investigations. The fact that the Examiner mentioned this made me think at the time that he, himself, might hold suspicions that there had been foul play, and that Jessup might have been made to commit suicide against his will.

And the fact that the files had been kept open for longer than the required period reinforced my own belief that Dr. Davis shared this opinion.

One of the most unusual disclosures in that file, Ann found, was that NO AUTOPSY HAD BEEN PERFORMED. I had known this previously and questioned Dr. Davis about it in a letter. He replied that it was because the body had been donated to the University of Miami School of Medicine.

To Ann, whose husband is a well-known banker in Miami, this explanation was not good enough.

"I can quote you," she told me, "from the Florida State Code, No. 406.11, which lists 15 circumstances where autopsies are required. And Jessup's case fits at least three of these: (1) He was a suicide. (2) He was not attended by a practicing physician. And (3) There certainly were unusual circumstances."

Ann discovered that the only tests made on the body were for blood alcohol and carbon monoxide. The alcohol test was negative, the other positive. No tests were made to determine if Jessup could have been under the influence of drugs. Nobody at the Examiner's office could offer Ann any explanation as to the lack of an autopsy.

The Mysterious "Doctor"

Other unusual factors about the Jessup case continue to haunt us:

For example, Sgt. Ted Obenchain, the homicide officer who investigated the death, told Ann, "The job was 'too professional.' And I've been on homicide a long time and I feel I can make such a judgment. For example, the ordinary suicide by monoxide poisoning doesn't take the time to wet down all the articles of clothing and to stuff them in the back window to make it more airtight.

"Most suicides use an ordinary garden hose. But the hose used in Jessup's car was larger in diameter, and similar to one on a washing machine. And it was not just shoved into the car's exhaust pipe. It was wired on. And all this had been done in broad daylight, just off a well-traveled road, at the height of the rush hour when traffic was leaving the park."

The water could hardly have been applied to the rags at the scene, or some second party had removed the evidence. The closest body of water was more than 200 yards away. Sgt. Ted Obenchain found no containers for carrying water to the car. Jessup's clothes were not wet, yet the rags used for stuffing the window were saturated with water.

In addition, there was the mysterious doctor who just "happened" to turn up at the death site to pronounce Jessup dead. While police were trying to revive Jessup by giving him oxygen, a man identifying himself as "Dr. Harry Reed" happened to walk through the park (though after closing time). He examined Jessup and pronounced him dead, though officially, the pronouncement had to come from the coroner's office.

Ann personally called and interviewed every doctor in the Miami telephone book, and later checked state records. None of the doctors had ever heard of Dr. Reed and he was not licensed in the state of Florida.

Another example was the fact that Jessup's wife, Rubye, refused to view the body, exclaiming that he could not be her husband, since she knew that he could not have committed suicide. Of course, this could be explained as due to extreme emotional trauma. But, Sgt. Obenchain had taken a personal interest in Mrs. Jessup and his wife offered to stay with her for a few days. She accepted the invitation, but asked her to leave after three days, but not before she had told Mrs. Obenchain about unusual telephone calls Jessup had been receiving prior to his death. These calls seemed to upset him, though he wouldn't tell her of the content. When Jessup was out and she answered the phone, the callers would hang up. The calls had ceased after Jessup's death. Ann, who believes that the death was by suicide, but that Jessup had been victimized by some kind of "mind control," viewed the phone calls as a part of that process.

Next example: The Medical Examiner's office recorded that the person who did identify the body was Leon A. Seoul. I told Ann that to my knowledge this name had never surfaced in UFO research, and she explained that the office believed the man to be a friend of the family.

Extensive inquiries in the local area failed to turn up any knowledge or trace of this person, who had an oriental-sounding name, in fact, the name of a Korean city. William Moore also checked on this, he told Ann, during his research for *The Philadelphia Experiment* and *The Roswell Incident,* but none of Jessup's relatives, near or distant, had ever heard of the person.

"No wonder," I told Ann, "that you believe in a conspiracy theory.

"First there was the doctor, or somebody posing as a doctor, hovering over the scene, just at the right time, wanting to make sure, it almost seems, that the suicide had been successful. Somebody possibly "getting to" Mrs. Jessup and influencing her not to view the body. Then another person, who could never be traced, performing the ritual of identification. And after all, we have no way of knowing that the body was actually that of Jessup. There are certainly many elements of a 'set-up' here."

Something That Might Be Big

But if a conspiracy did occur, Jessup subjected to "mind control" and made to commit the act, what was the motivation? Other facts Ann has accumulated during her investigations may point at such a motivation, and could give us some of the answers we are searching for.

Dr. Manson Valentine, a scientist and colleague of Jessup who lived in Miami, told Ann that he and his wife had been trying to reach the astronomer for three days prior to his death. They wanted to have him over to dinner and talk with him, for they believed him to be quite upset about something. Jessup had told them that he was "onto something big" (though Valentine did not believe that Jessup was upset enough to take his own life).

Six months previously, Jessup had visited the home of the late Ivan T. Sanderson in New York, and brought along one of the original annotated editions of his *The Case for the UFO*, which had been republished by the Varo Corporation. During the evening, Jessup asked Sanderson to bring three other persons (we don't know their names) into his private office. There he showed the four persons the copy which he had "re-annotated," or added his own notes to. He asked them to read it and then to lock it up for safe keeping "in case something should happen to me." While not disclosing what the notes contained, Sanderson stated that "after having read this material, all of us developed a collective feeling of a most unpleasant nature. And this was horribly confirmed when Jessup was found dead in his car."

Could Jessup have been privy to more information about the Philadelphia Experiment than those claims Allende had written to him? Ann believes he could have been a scientist assigned either to help plan the Experiment or help actually carry it out.

Although the CIA either could not or would not supply any information whatsoever, Ann acknowledges that the FBI was very cooperative and provided her with a complete report on Jessup, with very few deletions.

Why did the FBI conduct such an investigation? Jessup had applied for and had taken a government job. He worked for the government from May, 1943 until some time in 1944. *The Philadelphia Experiment took place on or about the middle of 1944.*

Whether by unlikely coincidence, or actual involvement, the time frame is just right.

As each year goes by, the possibility of exposing any foul play in the death of Jessup becomes more difficult to accomplish, and the perpetrators, if there were such persons, are safer from exposure. For instance, as soon as Ann became interested in the Jessup case, she began trying to track down Rubye Jessup. A year went by and then she was successful, but too late. Mrs. Jessup had died six months previously.

• • •

An Orchestrated Conspiracy?

Over a period of months, Gray Barker kept up his correspondence and actively accepted calls from Ann Ginzlinger, who really appeared to be trying to get to the bottom of Jessup's death. She had apparently decided a long while ago that the astronomer's death was part of an orchestrated conspiracy. She told Barker:

"Again, the question in my mind is not whether he took his own life. My question is—did he do it of his own free will, or was he driven to do it by a carefully orchestrated conspiracy by outside forces which wished to silence him and saw it to their advantage to have him commit the ultimate act himself while keeping their hands clean?

"In fact, when I discussed this with another investigator, William Moore, he told me, 'If this is true, you'd better be careful how you go about conducting your own investigations, for the type of creatures who would perpetrate such an act would not hesitate to repeat it if they thought somebody was ready to expose them!'"

There was also the question of the "Doctor" who appeared at the scene of the supposed "suicide" as well as the problem of who actually identified the body for the family. In his journals, now in the Clarksburg Public Library, can be found some of the actual questions Barker asked of the Florida woman:

• • •

GRAY: What about his wife, Rubye Jessup? Wasn't she present to identify the body?

ANN: She was present, but she adamantly refused to identify the body.

GRAY: Do you have any idea about why she refused?

ANN: She wouldn't accept the idea that it was her husband. She kept saying, "It can't be my husband!" And she refused to go and see the body.

The man who did identify the body is listed as "Leon A. Seoul." I have been unable to locate him, although feelers have been put out all over the United States.

GRAY: That name certainly doesn't ring a bell with me, as belonging to anybody with a UFO interest.

ANN: He was supposed to be a friend of the family.

GRAY: The name sounds Oriental.

ANN: Yes, that has struck me too. And I have another one for you—another person I've failed to track down. While the police were trying to revive Jessup by administering oxygen, a man who gave his name as "Dr. Harry Reed" happened to walk through the park. He examined Jessup and pronounced him dead. Of course, officially, Jessup had to be pronounced dead by the coroner's office.

GRAY: Was he a local doctor?

ANN: I have personally called and interviewed every Harry Reed in this city and none of these have ever heard of Jessup.

GRAY: It almost seems as if indeed foul play were involved, and whoever perpetrated it had their own doctor on the scene to make certain that Jessup was actually dead!

ANN: Perhaps to make sure that nobody revived him! What may have happened was that Jessup was found TOO SOON, by the park attendant.

GRAY: Was Jessup dead when the attendant found him?

ANN: We don't know, when he was first discovered. But by the time the police arrived, they could not detect any pulse or heartbeat.

GRAY: I assume he was familiar with suicides.

ANN: Oh yes. Although he had been on homicide for a short time, he was thoroughly qualified to make such a judgment. Also, most suicides use an ordinary garden hose. The hose used on Jessup's car was similar to one on a washing machine—the exhaust hose, five feet long and two inches in diameter. And it was not just shoved into the car's exhaust pipe; it was wired on. And all this had been done in broad daylight, just off a well-travelled road, at the height of the rush hour.

GRAY: Do you think the water was applied to the rags at the scene?

ANN: The closest body of water was more than 200 yards away. The police found no receptacles for carrying water. Jessup's clothes were not wet. Yet the rags used for stuffing the windows were saturated with water.

GRAY: My mind keeps gong back to Jessup's wife, Rubye. Have you been able to interview her?

ANN: I began my search for Rubye Jessup immediately after I began researching the Jessup case. I was unable to trace her down until more than a year later, when I learned she had died six months previously, in 1978.

GRAY: You indicate that she refused to view the body because she was so emotionally upset. This sounds logical enough—but do you think that "somebody" might have "got to her"?

Ann: This is Sgt. Obenchain's contention. Evidently he got personally involved in the case, possibly because of this idea. And he was very concerned about Mrs. Jessup's emotional state, the way she was taking it—so much so that he had his own wife go and stay with her for a few days. She told him Mrs. Jessup kept repeating over and over again, that it was not her husband. But, after three days, Mrs. Jessup asked her to leave, told her she no longer wanted to talk about it. This is one of the reasons the officer believed that somebody had got to her to shut her up.

Strange Telephone Calls

GRAY: Let's get to some possible motivation to get rid of Dr. Jessup. We know that prior to his death, he had been involved with Carlos M. Allende, who had written to him about the Philadelphia Experiment, and also apparently written some of the annotations in the book sent to the Navy. It's a fact that Jessup was called in to the ONR in Washington for questioning. Is it possible that Jessup had also been involved some way in the Experiment, beyond his passive role in receiving the letters and having written the book that was annotated?

ANN: I've believed that all along. I assume you're familiar with the late Ivan Sanderson's statements that Jessup got hold of a reprint of the annotated book and appended his own annotations?

GRAY: Yes. But what happened to this re-annotated copy?

ANN: I don't know. It was left at Sanderson's home. Of course Sanderson has died since and nobody has been able to locate it.

Six months before Jessup's death, he was a guest in Sanderson's home in New York, and that's when he left the copy. He also asked Sanderson to bring three other persons (we don't know just who) with them to Sanderson's private office. He handed them his re-annotated copy, asked them to read it and then to lock it up for safe keeping, "in case something should happen to me."

While not disclosing what the notes contained, Sanderson stated that "after having read this material, all of us developed a collective feeling of a most unpleasant nature. And this was horribly confirmed when Jessup was found dead in his car."

GRAY: Perhaps this re-annotated copy will surface some day and we can get a better idea as to just what Jessup knew that was so unpleasant.

ANN: I certainly hope so!

GRAY: During one of your conversations, you mentioned a rumor that Allende had visited Jessup shortly before his death...

ANN: It isn't a rumor. I have it on very good authority from a source I cannot name that Allende did visit Jessup three days before he died! Of course I have no idea what was discussed.

Another thing that bothers me very much is the series of telephone calls that Jessup received during the weeks just before his death. Rubye Jessup told Sgt. Obenchain's wife, while she was staying with her, about the calls which she sometimes took in his absence. They were from strange people who would-n't give their names, nor their business. She said that after Jessup took some of these calls he appeared to be greatly upset and distraught. She had the feeling he was being followed and that the phone was tapped.

GRAY: Could this have been the intelligence community?

ANN: It's entirely possible, and the calls could have been some way, possibly subliminal, of "getting into his mind."

• • •

Mind Control? Drugs? Hypnotism?

There have been many suggestions as to what—or who—actually killed Morris K. Jessup. The idea that drugs or some form of advanced hypnosis might have played a hand in his death has risen time and time again.

For example, a little known UFO writer by the name of Richard Ogden, living in Seattle, Washington, offered this shocking hypothesis:

"Now as for Jessup," Ogden states, "his suicide was a frame-up. Jessup fell victim to hypnotism. He was sent a tape recording that contained self-destruction suggestions. The tape employed hypnotic suggestions superimposed on music and mixed with white sound. No one can resist being hypnotized by sound waves. This is disguised hypnosis and it is foolproof. The white sound produces subliminal conditioning, a conditioning of the subconscious, a stimulus which affects the brain below the threshold of conscious awareness. There are certain sound wavelengths which are not audible to the conscious hearing but are heard by the subconscious.

"The equipment is officially known as Auralgesiac, audio analgesia, and connects to any high quality music system: tape recorder, phonograph. The white sound is used by physicians, dentists, and psychotherapists; it eliminates all pain and even major operations can be performed in hospitals with it and there is no pain. It eliminates the use of drugs.

"This means it produces a very deep state of hypnosis, and

it is the most powerful method for hypnosis known to medical science.

"Do you realize that someone could simply call you on the phone and when you answer, you are given a dose of white sound that puts you into a trance before you could even hang up. Your subconscious would be given suicidal thoughts and then you would go out and destroy yourself. Of course, first you would be told to write a letter to someone suggesting that you were about to commit suicide. This is what happened to Jessup. It is cold-blooded murder!

"No, I am not pulling your leg, and it is not too fantastic to be true! The equipment costs about $200 and can be obtained from a clinical supply company in New Jersey...."

Photo of Al Bielek seated in study of the late zoologist Ivan T. Sanderson, who was also a confidant of Dr. Jessup. Sanderson's own private copy of the Allende Letters vanished without a trace from his library.

Chapter Five
The Al Bielek Legacy

For many years, little in the way of new information came forward to support the contention that Jessup's death had been orchestrated. Nor for that matter was anyone collecting any previously unpublished data concerning the Philadelphia Experiment itself, and thus there was a noticeable lull in interest shown in these matters. Then one rather humid evening in 1989 a mysterious individual walked up to the microphone at Tim Beckley's annual New Age/UFO fest in Phoenix, Arizona, and shocked the many hundreds in attendance by claiming to have been a survivor of the Philadelphia Experiment. A hush fell over the auditorium as those present were glued to the edge of their seats in anticipation of some rather astonishing revelations. Initially, many thought that the mild mannered Bielek was a hoaxer, that he was not of "solid mind" and had actually concocted this rather outlandish story in order to gain attention.

Well, years have passed now and Al Bielek has traveled from one end of the continent to the other, and has been received with open arms as those who heard his tale come to realize that he is in all probability telling the truth as he remembers it.

As the months have worn on, Bielek has begun to remember more and more about what transpired back in 1943. He is the one who has been able to put most of the pieces of the puzzle together for us, because it is truly Bielek who was there when it all happened.

Alfred Bielek has come forward claiming to be a survivor of the horrible "invisibility" project conducted by the U.S. Navy.

Here is his own story in his very own words:

• • •

In 1947, there was a new political administration and a whole new administration of the military. The Joint Chiefs of Staff came into being. The Office of Naval Research was formed out of the old Office of Naval Engineering. We didn't have a Department of the Air Force, but that was coming about three years later. But we had a Pentagon and a whole hierarchy. So in 1947, somebody decided to take another look at this thing. Von Neumann was asked to take another look at this project to see what happened and whether anything could be salvaged. So he did.

Now, a number of other things happened in the meantime. This reopening of the project in 1947 occurred when I was no longer part of it. I was removed from the project and went elsewhere. The Navy put me on some other work until 1947, when they saw fit to remove me altogether.

Shipped to Montauk

Just before the first major UFO crash in the Roswell, New Mexico area (which was 7 July 1947), I was removed from the Navy. As I recall now, the details are quite clear. Because of where I was, I had full access to Navy files and records and a "black" vault to write a report for the Navy on the history of the development of the atomic bomb. I was at Los Alamos when they put me on a train and shipped me to Washington. They finally shipped me back to the East Coast to Montauk. At that point Montauk was a military base run by the Army and called Fort Hero. Fort Hero, in existence from sometime prior to World War I, was a military base for both Navy and Army. The Army installation included coastal defense guns. These big guns were on rail-carriers and held munitions storage and so forth. This went on through and after the period of World War II, and it was still operational as an army base in 1947.

Back in 1983 as Al Bielek

So they sent me there, and suddenly I was back in 1983. They pulled me back. I know this gets a little bit wild, but nonetheless this is what happened. They decided they had to really get rid of me. They didn't want to kill me—that's the eas-

An early photo of Al Bielek before he had full conscious recall of the part he played in the Philadelphia Experiment.

iest way to deal with something, to get rid of somebody who knows too much. But for reasons of their own they decided they couldn't do this. So they did a complete brainwash number on me. Sent me back to an earlier year. Built me in with memories from an earlier time and into another family called the Bieleks.

That's how I acquired the name Alfred Bielek. Even my birth certificate proved it. I have records as Alfred Bielek and absolutely no records as Edward Cameron, at least nothing that I could find anywhere. They've all been removed, erased, whatever you want to call it. They're very thorough at it.

And I grew up again, if you will. All the memories are there of growing up, going to engineering school, becoming a professional electronic engineer for thirty years and retiring from that around two years ago.

The Phoenix Project

Before I retired, however, a number of things occurred. In brief, I want to describe the Phoenix Project because I was involved in that also. It was a project which actually had its conception as a result of work that started at the end of World War II, in about 1947, at the time when they resurrected the Philadelphia Experiment. But it was separate from the Philadelphia Experiment at that point. The Phoenix Project started at Brookhaven National Laboratories in Long Island, and was particularly concerned with a group of immigrants who were scientists known prior to World War II. Research started on things like mind control and related projects. After I was disposed of, the UFO crashed in 1947 in the Roswell, New Mexico, area. A government team was set up to investigate this thing *after* the Army had picked it up and *after* the Army made its announcements (all of which are public record—that they had captured a UFO). They sent it to the Roswell papers and it is still part of a TV commentary and documentary out of Las Vegas, "UFOs as Evidence" by George Knapp.

One of the sequences in it deals with the actual history of what happened in 1947, the way they started a major coverup at that time. The crashed UFO on the ranch near Roswell contained dead aliens that looked more like locusts than humans. But the thing that really threw them into a tizzy and caused total pandemonium in Washington was the fact that there were human body parts within the wreckage. So who'd they call in to make their investigations? Dr. Vannevar Bush, the scientific Presidential advisor. Who was his assistant? Dr. John Von Neumann—also a matter of public record.

They investigated this crash. A second one occurred in 1947 and another one in 1948, and still another one in 1949. In 1949 they captured a live one, only the live one they captured wasn't like the dead ones. The live one they called EBE 1 was running around the fields. I'll have to conjecture a bit here because I never did ask them about it. I met Von Neumann later as Bielek and have some memory of some things. I never did ask him if he talked to this guy. I assume he did, because from someplace Von Neumann obtained the clues as to what was wrong with the Philadelphia Experiment.

Time Locks

The thing that was wrong and what had to be corrected sounds very simple in theory, but was very difficult to correct in practice. Every human being that is born on this planet, actually from the time of conception on, has what is called a set of time locks. The soul is locked to that point in the stream of time when conception takes place so everything flows forward at a normal rate of flow at the time function, mainly the fourth dimension. So you're part of society from day to day. When you wake up you wake up at the proper time, you know all the same people, everything's the same and you haven't slipped into another reality overnight. You are locked into a time span.

These locks stay with you your entire life. When you die they are gone and you are free to go elsewhere, so to speak, in time. You can reincarnate at another time, not necessarily later. You could go backwards. There are some records that indicate this. But those time locks are the things that were ruptured by the extreme power of the fields generated by Von Neumann's approach.

Von Neumann used four huge Teslacoil devices. They were

not the usual Tesla coils; Tesla built coils conically shaped. They were driven,in pairs, by each of the 75-rw generators operating at a fairly low frequency (pulsed). There were four rf transmitters, two megawatts each (cw); they also were pulsed at a 10% duty cycle. I won't go into the frequencies. Equivalent power was about 80 megawatts (pulsed). The antenna was on the ship's mast and the personnel on deck were almost next to that antenna. No one in history to that point had ever subjected a human being to such incredibly intense power fields, much less such incredibly intense magnetic fields. Nobody had any idea what would happen. Nobody gave it any consideration except Tesla, who knew something was going to happen.

Von Neumann finally agreed, probably something would happen. It did, of course. They wound up with insane people; they wound up with some people who lost their time locks, walked through nowhere and disappeared forever. They had others who were less fortunate. Four of them who had moved from their original position wound up in the steel deck. While the ship's fields were up there was no problem. When the fields collapsed and their time locks were gone, if they had, unfortunately, changed position, drifted and rematerialized in our dimension, our universe (because they were out of it) at a slightly different place or were unfortunate enough to be where the steel decking was, the steel of the deck literally melded with the molecules of their body. Not a very pleasant way to die. That is what happened.

Inventing a Computer to Solve the Problem

Now, the question was, what do you do to prevent it? The problem entailed understanding, which Von Neumann had to go back and do, basic metaphysics. Can you imagine a hard-headed Dutchman steeped in mathematics and with a particularly tough materialistic mind suddenly having to approach metaphysics? I'm sure that he was a little bit nauseated at first, but nevertheless he did his homework. And he found the problem. I do not know how he solved it, but he knew he had to have a computer.

In that day there were no real computers, no electronic

computers, so he literally invented it. He did it at the Institute between 1949 and 1951. The books are still on the shelves on the Von Neumann-Goldstein computer development, the theory, logic diagrams—I've seen them. In 1951 he had a computer that was fully operational in 1952. He built one for the Navy using a new approach to the project. Somehow he solved the time-lock problem, but I really don't know how.

The Fourth Test Leading to Project Phoenix

In 1953 they had another test: another ship, another crew. Fully successful. No problem with people walking through walls or disappearing or turning up in the back room of a bar that didn't exist in downtown Philadelphia (which is one of the stories). Everything worked properly. So what did they do? The Navy cancelled Project Rainbow and renamed it Project Phoenix, and it became part of the already ongoing Project Phoenix in another capacity, another guise.

That project continued onward for a number of years and eventually resulted in all the hardware which it has generated since—the Stealth hardware, the Stealth bomber (invisibility). They now have invisibility fields and shields for our large ships, the carriers. There is public information on this about our carriers disappearing off the radar screens and even from private aircraft following a carrier in the Pacific—just disappearing one day and three days later showing up 3,000 or so miles away on radar and again optically visible. So the problem, then, was solved, and Von Neumann, of course, went on to other things.

What happened after that is rather strange. The Phoenix Project continued onward. The aspects of mind control, which was one of the original functions of that project, were all under government control in the government laboratory at Brookhaven. Like all government laboratories, they must write monthly reports called progress reports. They've got them; they went someplace in Congress. Nobody knows exactly where, but someplace around 1958, somebody decided to read them. (Sometimes it takes Congress a long time to wake up.) They reacted: "Mind control? —who wants *this*? We don't want to have any part of it; they might use it on us. Cancel the project."

They did.

The scientists were thrown out of Brookhaven, so they went looking for a new home. Actually it was around 1967–1968 that this occurred, insofar as the mind-control project was concerned. At that point Fort Hero was already under Air Force jurisdiction for the Sage Project, which was, of course, the early warning radar in 25 stations around the perimeter of the United States. The Army people thought, "Well, it might be a good idea to have them out here and continue their research," so the scientists moved to Fort Hero. Eventually the Air Force abandoned that project because along came Dew Line and then the BEM Early Warning System. So all of these Sage projects went down. After that a lot of things happened. Basically they went into time travel and other projects, some of which we don't even know to this day.

The Monster Created by Project Phoenix

On the 12th of August 1983, Project Phoenix locked into the Philadelphia Experiment. What happened to the Phoenix project? It crashed that night, a night of horror in which a well-described monster looking much like an "abominable" snow-man, a Sasquatch, which was described (depending upon how panicked people were who saw it) as 12 to 30 feet high. It went around smashing buildings and people. So the director of the project at that time—it was Jack Pruett—said "We've got to shut this station down." And they again had the same problem we did; they couldn't shut it down by pulling the switch handles. They went outside and cut the power cables that were feeding the station. It didn't make any difference. The station kept running, but with no power feeding it. Pruett was very panicked himself, telling everybody, "Get out of here! I'll take care of it."

It is interesting to note that what happened there is almost exactly what Einstein himself warned about many years before that. He said, "if you create a machine with sufficient complexity and give it enough power, it will become intelligent of itself." And that apparently is what happened there. This machine called the Phoenix Project had a massive computer complex. It found out how to tap a power source—the Dirac sea, and fed its own energy in. It didn't need local power to run it. At that point the only way to shut it down was to destroy its brains, which means its computer connections, feed connections and modulators, and cut them to pieces. The brain no longer functioning, the machine went down; Junior, the monster, disappeared and that was the end of the Phoenix project— late that night of 12 August 1983.

There were two other aspects that are very important to this project and then I will go into a little more of the history.

Meeting My Brother 46 Years Younger

Why the August 12 date? We never did find that out at that period of time. We didn't really come up with the answer to that until after I came out of my brainwashing and my brother came out of his. My brother, by the way, to close the history on that, died in 1983, at which time he became a walk-in to another body, the *last* son of Alexander Cameron, Sr. (and his fifth wife) on August 12, 1963, which is a crucial date, and took over that body—kicked out the personality that was there, if you will. All of his memories today are basically from August 1., 1963.

In 1985 I was to make a visit to Long Island after meeting Duncan and a person he was working for who was running a laboratory on Long Island, Mr. Preston Nichols. I met them at the USPA conference in July, 1985. They invited me to come out and visit their lab on Long Island, which I did a month later. Preston took both of us to Montauk for the first time he thought (so far as our brainwashing was concerned, it was for the first time). "I have something I want to show you. I know you sense these things because you both seem to be rather sensitive individuals." So he took us out there. We sensed something really horrible and terrible on that base. We didn't know what it was, but we didn't like it.

After repeated visits I moved to Long Island in August, 1986. Staying there and working with both of these people every day, my memory started to come back about Montauk. They already had, both of them. Preston was part of it himself. That didn't bring back the memories of the Philadelphia Experiment, but it laid the groundwork.

The Movie

In August, 1984, a movie was released in the United States by EMI Thorn from England entitled *The Philadelphia Experiment*. This story was shot in the U.S. in 1982–83. They wanted to shoot outside the Phoenix Project terminal on Long Island, but the government wouldn't let them. So they went to Utah and did it there. They changed a few dates; they changed the 1983 date to 1984 and they changed the location to Utah. And they changed the date of the Philadelphia Experiment from August to October 1943. But the beginning of the movie is actually quite accurate. And it does portray two guys jumping off the ship (my brother and myself), falling into the future, going back and smashing the equipment, my brother going back to 1983 and myself remaining in 1943.

EMI Thorn, from what we were told, had had the script—or, should we say, not perhaps the script for the movie but the actual history of that project—in their files for decades. It's a long story, and I won't go into it, but they based their entire story on the emotions and the love interest, the girl in 1983, which makes a good movie but it did not adhere completely to the facts.

Three days before it was released the U.S. Government sent a note to EMI Thorn saying, "We do not want this movie released in the United States." EMI Thorn was on the horns of a dilemma: They had already given their release dates for the movie all over the U.S. They decided to play dumb and pretend they never got the letter.

So they did and the movie was released. It was in Sedona here in August, 1984, because I was here at that time. Friends of mine went to see it that night but didn't tell me about it. It was gone a week later. I didn't get to see it till many years later. Two weeks later it had been shown in New York, Chicago, Los Angeles, Phoenix, Philadelphia—there were lines around the block in Philadelphia. The government fired another letter to EMI Thorn that said, "We don't want that movie shown in the U.S. at all." EMI Thorn could not ignore the second letter and said,

"If you want it stopped, you get a court order." The U.S. Government said, "Yes, we will." And they did; they banned it by court order for two years. EMI Thorn obtained a counter-injunction and eventually had the first one removed. From that point on EMI has had a video available, and it is still available today in video stores. You may also see it on HBO and other cable shows; it is currently quite popular.

That is the history of the movie. It adheres quite well in many respects. Sidney Longstreet in the movie plays the scientist who was actually Dr. John Von Neumann. Von Neumann's assistant at that time was probably Gustaf Lebon, who does not show in the records at Princeton at all. Von Neumann does; he was on staff. They had a huge file on him. There are no records for Tesla having been there; I asked them why not. They said, "Simply because he was not on staff. We only keep records of people who were actually on staff, paid by the Institute." They said, "We have a lot of consultants come in here for awhile, do a project and then leave. We do not keep records on them." It was a legitimate answer. In any case, that is the end, basically, of two projects.

In January, 1988, I was up late one night watching HBO and at 4 o'clock in the morning I was about to turn in and they announced the next feature film of the evening would be *The Philadelphia Experiment*. My ears went up like the proverbial rabbit's, and I said, "Well, I'm going to see this. I have not seen it to date." So I stayed up the rest of the night until well in the morning watching it. It quite literally hit me like a bomb. While watching it I knew I had some part in this thing. Eventually the memories came back and I finally called my brother. (I had returned to Phoenix in March, 1987.) I said, "Hey, guess what? I was part of the Philadelphia Experiment." My brother says, "Yea, we know." I said, "What do you mean, you know?" He says, "We've known for a month and a half. We were waiting for you to find out without our telling you."

The interesting point about my brother's recollection is the fact that he had never seen the movie or video or read either of the two books on the Philadelphia Experiment. In the process of hypnotic regression, he had gone backward through his lifetime up to the point of August, 1963—and suddenly he was at August, 1943, on the *Eldridge*. And I was there. He knew we were both there, but he had not had the stimulus of the movie. That was the way I finally got it back. Much more has come back since.

Von Neumann remained part of the Phoenix Project. Actually, he was a consultant until it went down in 1983, and then he retired from the government, saying "I want nothing more to do with the government or any government projects. I am retiring, period." To set the record straight: The public record states that Von Neumann died of cancer in 1957. This is well known, well recorded; there was a funeral and all of this. But nothing could be further from the truth. He was part and parcel of that project and was director until 1977, when he started to suffer a problem with a split personality. He removed himself as director and the government said, "No, you've got to stick around." So he remained as a consultant. He is alive today—as far as I know, he's alive yet today—because I talked with him under this split personality in November, 1989, at his home in upper New York State.

The August 12 Date

August 12 is very significant for a reason that eluded us until about 1988. The human system has three biorhythms; that's well established. It turns out that the earth has its own biorhythm fields—four of them. This was not known in the forties; it was not even known in the early eighties. This was discovered by a friend of mine doing some research with rf receivers and noise background. When he thought he saw some kind of a strange correlation, he obtained government money to research this thing and finally hit the jackpot after doing a full computer correlation. He found out that the earth has four biorhythms, *which all peaked out on one date:* August 12, 1943, 1963, 1983, and twenty years in either direction, forward or past ad infinitum. The actual date of the 12th may vary slightly plus or minus half a day, because those peaks aren't absolute, just like the human-body ones. But they do peak out in a rough 24-hour period. And there was the synchronization between the two experiments, which had already provided enough of the higher level of field energy in order to cause lock-up. The other missing point I'll go into later.

The Allende Letters

In 1955 a very strange thing happened. A book arrived in the office of Admiral Firth, the Office of Naval Research in Washington, entitled *The Case for the UFO* written by Morris K. Jessup, an internationally known astronomer. In the margins were all kinds of handwritten footnotes, which reportedly were written by three gypsies—later they claimed there was only one, Carlos Allende. A series of letters started to arrive at Morris K. Jessup's mailbox. When the book arrived, there was knowledge in it dealing with outer space. We did not yet have the first satellite up, much less the first rocket, which was two years later—the Russian Sputnik, launched into orbit. An office staff, a team, was set up under the auspices of George Hoover, the Office of Naval Research. I talked with Mr. Hoover, still alive (at least when I last talked with him) and in retirement in California. I asked him about this and that and the Philadelphia Experiment. He said, "Oh yes, the Philadelphia Experiment. A lot of people don't realize there were many experiments going on at that time," he said. "But it was very interesting from the standpoint that I became involved with it because of the Allende letters, and we did a major investigation. We went through the files and found a number of medical reports. The medical report made as a result of the investigations *after* the fact of the experiment, were very interesting. That was the first time in history people had been exposed to such very powerful electromagnetic fields, and the results in the reports led to some other things." He admitted to me on the phone that the Philadelphia Experiment did occur—he had read the files. And he had been part of this.

Well, this goes on. Basically, Jessup became heavily involved. Hoover invited him to Washington three times to question him. Jessup knew nothing about the matter except the letters from Allende, and he became interested in the project. By 1959 he had quite a file himself. He called a friend of his one afternoon in Dade County, Florida, and said, "I think I have the answer to this thing. I'm going to be over there in about an hour. I'll bring my file with me." This was in the afternoon of that particular day. He never arrived. The next morning his dead body was found in his car in a park in Dade County with a hose from the exhaust going in the window. Dead of monoxide poisoning and, of course, no briefcase, no file notes, nothing. And this thing blew up in the press like you wouldn't believe. Just exactly what the government did *not* want. So as a result of that they learned something. If a person is talking about classified projects and is in the public view and has a public following, they've automatically invoked the martyrdom clause. Mr. Jessup paid the price.

Books on the Subject

There have been a number of books written about this subject. The first book written on the Philadelphia Experiment was entitled *Thin Air,* a totally fictional book by two "unknown" authors, published in 1978. It basically tells the story of two retired sailors having terrible nightmares of being on fire and on a ship. The plot proceeds to track down the history of the Philadelphia Experiment, but in a fictional style. The next book, *The Philadelphia Experiment* by Berlitz and Moore, came out in 1979. Then there is another book, *How You Can Explore Higher Dimensions in Space and Time* by T.B. Pawlicki, 1989. It does not detail specifically the Philadelphia Experiment, but it does document certain other theoretical aspects. It may be out of print.

In the book Pawlicki goes into basic structures to explain our three-dimensional universe and how we go beyond them, seen here on a flat surface. You start with a point; one dimension is a line. Two dimensions are represented by a triangle (being the smallest expression of an enclosed two-dimensional structure on a piece of paper). And you can draw the projections to show a three-dimensional structure. You can then draw further to show four dimensions (hard to visualize, unfortunately).

One of the other aspects involved here is trying to show what happens when you accelerate beyond a speed "limit" which Einstein was quoted as calling c. The textbooks say that Einstein said c was the limiting speed of anything in this universe, and that if you accelerate a mass to the speed of light, it will lose one of its dimensions; it will become a flat object. Not strictly true. It rotates in a space-time continuum; it doesn't lose a dimension; it only *seems* to lose a dimension from our reference. As this chart and some of the text in the book explains as you accelerate energy-wise to c you start to truncate and to spiral. The bottom is zero acceleration of velocity. The first right quadrant is c, the second quadrant is c squared. The third quadrant is c cubed. If you close this spiral down in terms of space-time, the energies become tighter.

Pawlicki's Toms of Time

The most important aspect, however, which Pawlicki goes into in his book, is the so-called torus of time. Based on this, one can begin to understand what went on—that is, if you have a mind for it either mathematically or by visualization. Einstein said flatly that there is no such thing as a straight line in our universe. If you start from a point (it doesn't make any difference what direction you go) and aim at a point in a straight line (as you may think of a straight line) far enough, you will wind up in full circle and hit yourself in the back. The same is also true of time. It is also in a closed circuit, what we sometimes call the torus of time. What does this mean? This thing is huge; it's not a small structure, and this, of course, is only a mathematical representation. It means that in the center of this donut shape time flows at a linear rate, but it also flows in a spiral around the periphery. This is speaking mathematically. If you go from the center to an outside edge, you are in an alternate reality. If you progress around that rim you go into alternate realities parallel to your own.

This is an extremely important point not only in terms of mathematics but also in terms of what happens when something like the *Eldridge* or some other object disappears. The *Eldridge* moved in time, but it actually moved into hyperspace. It was not intended that it should move in time, but only rotate the time field to gain invisibility. The theoretical aspects here begin to give some idea of what is going on, because you can literally construct this. With the right hardware you can achieve time rotation. What does it take? It takes a little misnomer in the way of energy and theory, less than you might expect. Without boring you, it takes a sixth-order field. Somewhat hard to explain, but we can say this much: The *Eldridge* was capable of generating a sixth-order energy field, and the Phoenix Project, an eighth-order field. Years later, as Von Neumann used to argue, the *Eldridge* generated a sixth-order field and the Montauk project generated an eight-order field. Where did the other four come from? They *had* to have twelve for the *Eldridge* to go into hyperspace.

It was not recognized for some time what happened. First of all, the Montauk Project was not operating on 22 July 1983, according to log books. On August 1 an order came down that was unusual—in fact, unprecedented: Montauk would become operational 24 hours a day around the clock for an unknown period into the future. So it was put into that kind of operation. It took some very abstruse theory; the system that was generated by the function of Montauk was capable, with the power and the functions they had, to go to plus or minus infinity in terms of time. In other words, they could circumnavigate the entire torus of time within a little less than 24 hours. And in doing so they added an order of reality which was impressed upon the pulse-forming networks and the special banks they had for the modulator system. They were able to add another order of reality every day, so after five days they could make it to the twelfth order or beyond. And with that, plus the very critical date of 12 August in 1943 and 1983 when both systems were online, they locked in. What happened when they locked in? They had to go beyond the experiments. It actually opened a hole in hyperspace forty years wide.

Phoenix Project Enabled Invasion of the Grays

Now, if you want a little history of UFOs and problems with ETs at the present time, a mass invasion took place, which Cooper has mentioned. There was a massive invasion of the Grays during the period in the early fifties onward. The invasion is over, because they're already here. The indications are that they came from another space-time continuum, a reality other than the one we consider as our universe. They had to have a way of getting in, in massive numbers. This was their way: This entire project, the two coupling together, as I view it now today with the data I have, was generated for the specific purpose of creating a hole in time-space to allow a massive invasion of earth, into our reality, into our system. That took a great deal of knowledge and a great deal of control by extraterrestrial intelligences.

To my knowledge there are no ETs involved in the functioning of the Philadelphia Experiment. There were a great many involved in the functioning of the Phoenix Project. The basic technology that we had was inadequate. We had already created time machines by 1970 but not the capability of boring "holes in space," as Dr. Sagan called them—which means the capability of going not only through time but space anywhere in the universe. That was the function of Montauk; and it took a technology that was beyond us generated and provided by a group of aliens that worked there for over ten years converting their technological data to our IBM 360 formats because we didn't have the computers in those days that could handle it, other than by manual conversion. They did it. Today we could match their computers with the Cray 2, certainly with the Cray 3. But Cray 3 did not exist in those days. So we found the means to create this monstrosity called the Phoenix Project. They wanted it and found the means to create their entrance to our universe.

Phantom Ship the USS *Eldridge*.

Chapter Six
Further Details
About Al Bielek

Unlike those who seem not in the least bit anxious to reveal their "sources" or to tell "all they know" about certain aspects of either the UFO mystery or the Philadelphia Experiment, Al Bielek seems more than willing to lay it all "on the line."

When Ken Crowley flew from Solola, Guatemala to San Diego to attend a UFO conference, little did he realize that he would get to know first hand one of the speakers at the convention. For Crowley was able to sit down with Al Bielek for a period of several hours and quiz him from "top to bottom" about matters that had changed his life.

As far as we know, this is one of the few lengthy interviews to be held with Bielek to this date. No doubt other questions will arise, and he has promised to answer them the best he knows how, adding to what appears to be his sincerity in this regard:

• • •

Until recently, very little has been known about the top secret Navy Department project referred to as the Philadelphia Experiment, a project to make objects invisible. Even a film bearing the same name produced in the 1980s divulged very little about the unusual testing involving the lives of many servicemen and a technology that can only be described as highly advanced or alien. Scientist Al Bielek assisted in developing the project and special equipment on board the destroyer *Eldridge* and operated it during the tests in 1943. He is one of the few who lived to tell about it.

Alfred Bielek was originally born Edward Cameron on August 4, 1916. He received a Ph.D. in physics at Harvard before joining the "90 day wonder" officers training program in 1939. Today, he is an imposing figure, 6'3" tall, with a quick mind and articulate speech. But he is a quiet, retiring man and somewhat reclusive, living alone as a bachelor in Atlanta, Georgia. When approached, one finds him remarkably accessible and open to discuss his experience, but difficult to follow at times when his crisp scientific mind delves deep into the inner workings of the experimental hardware and the complexities of time travel.

The Philadelphia Experiment began as early as 1931, as a feasibility study to make objects disappear, headed by none other than Yugoslavian born Nicola Tesla. Because of the war in the 1940s, the goal was expanded to make mine sweepers and a battleship invisible.

The original team included John Hutchinson, Dean of the University of Chicago, and an Austrian physicist named Dr. Emil Kurtenaur. The knowledge of Dr. David Hilbert, whose theories described multiple realities and multi-level universes, and physician T. Townsend Brown, were essential to the project. This research was funded from the beginning by the U.S. Navy.

In 1934, the project moved to the east coast, to the Institute for Advanced Studies at Princeton, of which Albert Einstein was a member. Although Einstein's Unified Field Theory was used as the basis for the experiment, he never participated directly in the group's effort.

The organization was later joined by Dr. John Eric Von Neuman, who had studied at the University of Berlin and the University of Hamburg in Germany. Tesla was briefly absent from the group until the late thirties because of other projects, finding it necessary to spend time in Washington, D.C. to enhance his ongoing relationship with President Franklin D. Roosevelt.

It was during these years that Tesla was said to have invented a special radio device capable of reaching and maintaining contact with extraterrestrial beings on another planet. A friend of Tesla reports that this contact continued on a daily basis. It was alleged that Tesla himself was an alien from Venus. He was the only scientist ever known who could visualize an entire experiment in his head, create the hardware, then make it work the first time. "From an earthly standpoint," says Bielek, "that is not humanly possible."

To effect the goal of making an object disappear, it was considered necessary to break the time reference that binds the three dimensional reality. The fourth dimension is called a linear time vector. The fifth dimension, they determined, consisted of a rotating locus or corkscrew that determines the flow rate of time. To break the time reference, the group created a pulsating and non-pulsating generator system to enter and overcome the fourth and fifth linear time vectors. By changing an object's time, they could thereby cause the object to appear and disappear.

Al Bielek's recall of both his personal experience and the intricate workings of the hardware developed by himself and the team to dissolve objects the size of battleships by changing their time is truly remarkable. It was a memorable experience listening to Bielek tell his story during the 1992 UFO Conference in San Diego, and follow through with in-depth personal conversations.

KENN CROWLEY: When did the first Philadelphia test experiment really take place?

AL BIELEK: In 1936, there was a test considered partially successful. In 1940, the second test, they applied coils and a generator to a tender at the Brooklyn Navy Yard. This was fully successful, but without personnel on board. The entire project was classified as Project Rainbow.

Even during this period, Tesla understood that the ship had its own time lock, while each of its personnel had their own individual time lock reference. To compute all that using ordinary long-hand mathematics could have taken years. Computers in those days were nonexistent, and in order for the experiment to work fully manned, the experiment had to include data on the zero time reference of both ship and personnel.

CROWLEY: When did you actually join the project?

BIELEK: Well, both my brother, Duncan, and I joined together. My brother Duncan also received a Ph.D. in physics from the University in Edinburg, Scotland, and together we entered a Naval officers training program in Providence, Rhode Island. After graduation, we were assigned to the Institute for Advanced Study at Princeton.

In 1940, after the first successful unmanned experiment, we were transferred to the *U.S.S. Pennsylvania.* During this tour of duty, the ship was placed into drydock for repairs in Pearl Harbor. That was in October of 1941, and we took leave to San Francisco. The Office of Naval Engineering suddenly cut us new orders. We were told that Pearl was to be attacked by the Japanese and the government didn't want two men of our caliber to be on board. We continued our tour of duty in San Francisco, shuffling papers until January, 1942, when we rejoined the Institute at Princeton.

CROWLEY: When did the project officially shift into a military operation?

BIELEK: It was when Duncan and I returned to the project in 1942 that it clearly became a military endeavor. The war was in full swing and the government was in hopes of creating invisible ships to sail by, unseen, and destroy enemy craft. The project fell under a series of military deadlines. A war was on, and the technology was needed right away. Tesla was extremely sensitive about the personnel involved and knew that the experiment was not ready for a manned operation. During the first manned test on board a battleship (donated by Roosevelt), in March of 1942, Tesla detuned the operation and of course it was a failure. Tesla was removed as chief of operations and replaced by Dr. John Von Neuman, who redesigned the approach. Tesla turned up dead ten months later in his hotel room in New York in January, 1943.

CROWLEY: Are you able to describe the technology of the inner workings of such a machine?

BIELEK: Tesla had used what is called an analog approach, where all equipment was left continuously on, modulated with four different very complex waveforms using two modalities. One modality was the power generator at a specific frequency. It was used to drive four non-typical Tesla coils. The generator sat on the deck with its drive motor. In the later *Eldridge* version, two generators plus four RF transmitters of two megawatts each were used. There was a special antenna on the mast of the *Eldridge* to transmit the RF waves.

With two megawatts of power, Tesla knew there would be personnel problems. No human mind or body had ever been subjected to this much energy.

Upon assuming control in 1942, Von Neuman redesigned the system and later requested a new ship. This was the DE-173 *Eldridge*. He took what is known as a digital approach and put two large generators, 75 KVA each, in the hold. The number two gun turret was left off entirely, replaced by an eight megawatt diesel powered generator and master pulse oscillator. Von Neuman's system produced a central rotating electromagnetic field at a critical frequency to interact with the second time vector. This rotated the position of the time field in relation to the ship and was what allowed the ship to become invisible.

CROWLEY: What were some of the main difficulties and problems the group ran into?

BIELEK: The rotating time field was not the problem. The problem was regulating the power requirements. No human body had ever been exposed to 20 megawatts of RF pulse power only 75 feet away from the antenna. Some knew the results could be disastrous because the maximum power exposure could not exceed 100 milliwatts per square centimeter of surface skin. This is known as the "Heatimo Effect" unit. In subsequent studies, it has long since been learned that the maximum safe exposure level, in consideration of neurological window effect, is 100 microwatts per square centimeter. The Russian standard is typically set at 10 microwatts per square centimeter.

Effects on the brain, they discovered, would come from the critical window frequencies. Many years would elapse before the "window frequency" effect of neural brain resonance would be understood. These effects are only being fully explored and charted since the 1970s.

Select volunteers were specially trained by my brother, who was head of the enlisted man program to operate some of the equipment and the ship.

In 1943, Von Neuman realized there still could be a personnel problem, but the deadline had to be met under the auspices that a greater good would be created by sacrificing a few lives now.

CROWLEY: When did the first manned experiment take place and what happened?

BIELEK: The experiment was attempted in July of 1943, but there were complications. My brother and I ran the equipment in the hold below deck and below the waterline. For 20 minutes, we became invisible both visually and to radar, but there was far too much power and it made the crew on deck very ill.

CROWLEY: How long was it before the next attempt?

BIELEK: On August 12, 1943, at 09:00 hours, in the Philadelphia harbor, they decided to take a modified approach and turned the power down to attain only radar invisibility. The Brass decided that radar invisibility would be enough if they could proceed past the enemy undetected for the remainder of World War II. For the first 60 seconds, the observers could see the ship through a green mist, then they lost radio contact. Four hours later it returned to the same location. Some of the ship was damaged, while other parts were missing. Missing mind you—we had to ask ourselves what happened to the missing equipment, but no one had any concrete answers.

As the experiment wound down, my brother and I walked on deck to see all hell breaking loose. It was horrible. Two sailors were embedded in the deck, two embedded in the bulk head. One sailor had his hand embedded in the steel, which had to be amputated in place. He was the only one who lived and now has an artificial hand. The rest of the crew on deck was in a mentally deranged state of hysteria and insanity.

CROWLEY: What did you do during the crisis?

BIELEK: In the emergency, we tried to shut the machinery down, but the power switches would not bulge, so we quickly decided to jump overboard. Then we got the surprise of our lives. Instead of landing in the water as you might think, we landed standing up in a military installation in Montauk, New York at Fort Hero—and not in 1943 as one might presume, but 40 years into the future. It was now 1983.

When we came to our senses, we were met by a much older Dr. John Von Neuman working in something called the Phoenix Experiment, the great grandchild of the Rainbow Experiment. Here in Montauk, we discovered ourselves in an alien-military underground installation with an advanced system of computers and other very modern and sophisticated equipment. We could hardly believe it. We watched helicopters and a Boeing 747 jetliner fly overhead and even got a taste of watching color TV. Remember, none of those things existed in the 40s.

CROWLEY: I've heard there may have been a UFO involved at that time. Would you comment on that?

BIELEK: Yes. Between August 4th and 12th, just before this test, we sighted three UFOs hovering above the *Eldridge*. One saucer had been sucked into our vortex and landed underground but at an earlier time. This UFO was dismantled at Montauk.

CROWLEY: So here you are in 1983. Did you and your brother just stay in that time zone?

BIELEK: No. We were only there for about 12 hours. Von Neuman told us that the Philadelphia Experiment and the Phoenix Project had become locked in a hyperspace bubble, and that it would be necessary for them to return us to the *Eldridge* to destroy the equipment. It was the only way. Von Neuman admitted they had created an artificial reality that could not be controlled.

CROWLEY: How was that done?

BIELEK: We were placed in a time tunnel and the juice turned on. When we returned to the *Eldridge* we saw people burning on deck and general mass hysteria. We immediately went in to the control room and axed the equipment. As the machines were winding down—but before the field actually collapsed—Duncan again jumped overboard and landed back in 1983. He aged at approximately one year per hour and quickly died of old age. With the alien space-time technology, Duncan was reborn in 1951, sired by our father, Alexander Cameron, and his fifth wife. I remained on the ship and returned to 1943. Amazingly enough, my physical condition seemed unimpaired.

CROWLEY: With such drastic results, was that the end of the experiment?

BIELEK: No. In October of the same year, there was one last unmanned attempt that was also a disaster.

CROWLEY: What direction did you take subsequently?

BIELEK: I was thereafter assigned to work in a Los Alamos laboratory, but my involvement in the experiment had changed me and I began talking too much. I was emotionally affected by what had happened to me and my brother and the crew and I couldn't help complaining about how things had been handled. In essence, I became a security risk, and was charged with espionage in July, 1947. I was arrested, handcuffed and taken to Washington, D.C. where the charges were dropped. But I was still considered too dangerous to be allowed to run around and shoot my mouth off.

CROWLEY: What was the government's reaction?

BIELEK: It was at this point that they performed the great-granddaddy of all goodbyes. They took me to Fort Hero at Montauk toward the back of the base, where they had me stand in the center of a grass plot surrounded by a donut-shaped cement wheel embedded in the ground. The grass circle was about 25 feet in diameter. They then told me not to move. I was sent forward in time to 1983, where I was picked up by Von Neuman, who said the government had ordered him to "bury" me.

With alien technology developed under the Phoenix experiment, I was sent back to 1927 as a one-year-old child whose parents believed their infant son had died at birth, and Mr. and Mrs. Arthur Bielek.

The Montauk technicians were warned by the aliens not to physically regress anyone beyond the age of 21 years old or there would be genetic problems, but they did it anyway. As I grew up during my second childhood, I had a very difficult time. I grew like a weed to more than six feet tall when I was only 12 years old.

CROWLEY: Do you have any idea as to where this physical regression activity might have been developed?

BIELEK: Physical age regression had its genesis in the Hughes Medical Research Center in Miami, Florida, starting in the 1950s. By the early 70s, they were consistently regressing "old age" from 75 years old to 55 or less. By the time the Phoenix Project was on line in 1975, the U.S. government/alien technology enabled actual physical age regression from 65 to 25 years of age with no loss of mental ability.

CROWLEY: What kind of life did you lead as Alfred Bielek?

BIELEK: As a Bielek, I grew up very differently than in my first life. I became interested in electronics and joined the Navy in 1945, still with no recollection of my past lifetime as Cameron. Finally in 1988 I saw the movie *The Philadelphia Experiment*, which caused many of the old memories to flood in on me. Brainwashing does not last forever and many things began to bleed through. I phoned my brother and began talking about our life together in 1943. My brother responded, "It's about time. We've been waiting for you."

CROWLEY: You mentioned that when you were advanced in time to 1983, you suddenly became part of the Phoenix Experiment. What was that project?

BIELEK: In 1947, the Phoenix Experiment resumed work on the Philadelphia Experiment at Brookhaven, New York, resurrecting much of the old equipment. The project would research mind control, invisibility and time-space manipulation. They employed mind-control methods similar to those used by the Nazi's in the 1940s. Remember, we picked up a lot of German scientists after the war. Both Dr. Werner Von Braun and Dr. Hermann Untermann brought over some of the German "know how" for the time travel experiments.

CROWLEY: How was the Phoenix Experiment funded?

BIELEK: For the first 20 years, the Phoenix Project, while at Brookhaven National Laboratories, was financed with U.S. tax money through Congress. Then the government cancelled it in 1968, because of Congressional investigation into funding.

The project moved to Montauk to continue time-tunnel, time travel and invisibility experiments. They were particularly interested in developing a "backpack" invisibility kit. Funding at Montauk came from buried Nazi gold bullion and laundered through the I.T.T. Corporation.

CROWLEY: Is it true there were alien beings involved in the project?

BIELEK: Yes. Aliens were directly involved in the Phoenix Experiment from the beginning of phase three at Montauk. Eventually, the Phoenix Experiment intended to take a time-tunnel approach to space-time travel, visit Mars, the moon, other planets in the solar system as well as other parts of our galaxy, with the power to move both backwards and forwards in time. We needed the help of aliens to understand it all and believe me, we accomplished every objective.

CROWLEY: Do you have any idea who these beings were and where they were from? Who supplied the technology?

BIELEK: Beings from the Orion Confederation controlled the operation. The Leverons and the Orion Confederation supplied the technology along with a group from Sirius A and some grays. There were also beings from Antares that were humanoid aliens not distinguishable from ordinary humans.

CROWLEY: Do you know how these time-change experiments worked?

BIELEK: During earlier phases of the experiment, the time-tunnel was steered with computers. Later we used psychics. They sat a psychic in one of their off-planet designed chairs and hooked wire patches at special probe points in his head to sense the correct psychic state. The energy of the psychic was relayed first to an alien Sirian computer, which then transferred the impulses to our Cray One, then into our IBM 360 computer. With this setup they could steer the system anywhere they wanted to go and the Phoenix setup had to be in place in 1983 for us to return to the *Eldridge.*

CROWLEY: Let me understand this correctly—were you working on the Phoenix project as Bielek when you and your brother landed there as Camerons in 1983?

BIELEK: That's correct. According to Von Neuman, there

was a small conflict in 1983. We had a paradox in time with our landing there from 1943, because we were already there in Montauk working on the Phoenix Experiment. Von Neuman knew that we should not meet up with ourselves in a time loop, and that it might be a disaster. There were many things Von Neuman did not understand so they kept us apart from our other selves.

When we returned to the *Eldridge,* we did not remember the Phoenix. It wasn't until later that our memories returned.

CROWLEY: Do you have any reason to believe that the aliens had anything to do with the Philadelphia Experiment?

BIELEK: Looking back, I would have to say, yes, although no one can ever be sure. Remember, there was a UFO sucked into the vortex that landed at Montauk. From the program's inception, Tesla was reported to be in contact with aliens by radio on a daily basis. When one examines the facts, it's only been since the 1940s that there has been such a large number of people abducted. There were a few UFO crashes and retrievals before the 1940s, but since then there have been many more, particularly since the development of radar.

To me, it looks like the entire Philadelphia Experiment was an alien conspiracy to create a 40-year-wide time rift to allow the passage of millions of alien grays into our time zone. In retrospect, one wonders if it was only Grays of the smaller variety that came through, since reptilians from the Orion and Oraco variety ran the Phoenix operation. I find it strange that this experiment closed down in August of 1983 just after the Philadelphia project's problems were solved. I also think the aliens were using the Phoenix to do their own manipulations, to say nothing of our own government's interests and manipulations.

CROWLEY: Whatever happened to Von Neuman? Do you think he's still alive?

BIELEK: The government claims that Von Neumann died in 1957. Not so. He was there at Montauk in the 1980s and later I discovered evidence that this illustrious scientist had written books dating up to the 1980s. It was all there in Princeton when I dropped in to enhance my memory and ran a computer check on him. He had written six more books dating into the 80s.

CROWLEY: What is the 20 miles of underground construction at Montauk, which runs under Fire Island, being used for today? With a record and range of such amazing accomplishments, it seems highly unlikely that the government just destroyed all that information and technology?

BIELEK: There are some questions I can't answer.

CROWLEY: I certainly appreciate your time, Mr. Bielek. One last thing: Through all these amazing years, do you have any regrets?

BIELEK: I guess. As Edward Cameron I married in 1943. My wife was already pregnant and I had a son born in February of 1944. 1947, I vanished without a trace. I know it was unbearable for them. My wife looked for me for years. Today, after extensive investigation on my part, I believe she was killed in an automobile accident in 1958, and I know that my son was reared by my Aunt in New Mexico. I have good reason to believe he is still alive today and looking for me.

Author's Conclusions: There are few men like Al Bielek walking the planet. It is no small wonder that he is still alive. When observing what our government capabilities were in the 40s to the 80s, normal curiosity makes one ponder over what they are into now. Bielek states that the government scrapped the Phoenix Project in 1983. The government claims that Von Neuman died in 1975.

Al Bielek has co-produced a book with Brad Steiger entitled *The Philadelphia Experiment and Other Conspiracies* and produced videocassettes one and two through Star Productions Corporation. He spends much of his time writing and travelling to UFO conferences as a guest lecturer, to make sure everyone knows that the Philadelphia Experiment really did take place. Hearing the story first-hand leaves no doubt in one's mind that this science fiction-like experience is one of the most remarkable realities of our time.

LIQUID WHICH CAUSES INVISIBILITY PROVED IN USE

SPARTANBURG, S.C., Dec. 10—(AP)—The Herald-Journal said in a copyrighted story today that a Spartanburg chemist has announced discovery of a substance which, when applied like paint, renders material objects invisible at a distance beyond 100 feet.

The newspaper quoted the chemist, Max Gardner, as saying the substance had been demonstrated on an airplane which was flown above a field near here. No part of the plane could been seen after it reached an altitude of 100 feet, Gardner said.

The Herald-Journal reported Gardner declined to describe the nature of the substance, but did say that its basic ingredient was ordinary graphite. The story said the chemist stumbled upon his discovery while seeking a substitute for aluminum.

Gardner said war department officials had been notified of the discovery and that army experts would come here this week to witness a demonstration.

Clipping submitted by Tom Beech, who says the story originally appeared in newspapers in 1938 or 1939.

It was from the highly classified Philadelphia Navy Yard that the USS *Eldridge* vanished into time and space (Photo circa World War II).

Chapter Seven
Return To Montauk

One of the most open, friendliest individuals who you are ever likely to meet is a fantastic artist and businesswoman by the name of Helga Morrow, who also just so happens to be an incredible psychic and channel, having had her share of UFO and out-of-body experiences.

A truly enlightened person, knowledge seems to run in the family, for Helga's father was none other than Dr. Fred A. Kueppers, a German-born engineer who defected to the U.S. during World War II.

Though I hate to repeat myself—I revealed Helga's full account about her dad in my previous book, *The Controllers*—I think it's necessary to backtrack just a bit and summarize the work of her deceased scientist father in order to lead up to some absolutely marvelous revelations that will be new to most of us.

"I have learned from various sources that my father was one of the scientists who worked on the Philadelphia Experiment," Helga recently stated for the record. "He also invented the timing device for the A-bomb; had been chosen by the bomb scientists to represent them to Harry Truman, asking him NOT to drop the bomb; had invented the mathematical formula that brought the astronauts back from space; had designated the miniaturized electrical system of Sputnik, the first space launching; had worked on Project Blue Book/Black Book (concerning UFOs); had initiated the use of aluminum wiring to replace the heavier wiring in World War II planes; had worked with mind warfare, using psychics to communicate

95

Entrance to prison where experiments were conducted on three unfortunate enough to be involved in the Montauk Project.

with astronauts; and had trained extraterrestrials to fit into human society."

Helga says she, herself, witnessed him performing what to him were "simple" experiments involving teleportation and levitation.

"When I was in the second or third grade, I watched him hang up an award from RCA in his room. I asked, 'Why did you get this award?' He told me it was too lengthy for him too go into. He said it was an award for an experiment in time, and then proceeded to put two ashtrays on his bed, and through simple gestures and explanations, show how two objects could transpose in time and return the same way. Then he took me into the cellar, where he put some steel shaving in a cigar box with a large U-shaped magnet taped underneath. He gently tapped the steel shavings, and to my amazement, two distant series of concentric circles gradually appeared. He then simplified this by saying that if one could transpose these circles, one could transpose time."

At one point, Dr. Kueppers told his daughter that he had worked with Tesla, Einstein, Von Braun, Von Neuman and many others. When he died—apparently under mysterious circumstances—Helga became convinced that his real body was not in the coffin, and to this date his actual grave site cannot be located and there are no grave records.

Several months following his supposed "passing," Dr. Kueppers appeared to Helga and told her he was not dead at all, but only living in "another dimension in time!"

One of the things that Helga Morrow eventually discovered was that her renowned father was also part of the so-called "Montauk Project." Desperately wanting to find out as much as she could about what went on in this Long Island town as an offshoot of the Philadelphia Experiment, Helga made arrangements to meet Peter Moon and Preston Nichols, authors of *Montauk Revisited*, (Sky Books, Box 769, Westbury, NY 11590), which is often thought of as the only authentic source of information on what went on in this quiet, little fishing community in the way of warping time and space for the benefit of the American military.

Because they then both lived in Arizona, Helga teamed up with Alfred Bielek and flew to New York to take a look at what remains of the underground complex of buildings that housed the Long Island branch of the Philadelphia Experiment.

Helga leaves little doubt that her trip to Montauk was a very fruitful one.

"During my trip, I was introduced to Preston Nichols, who worked there as a scientist in the now totally dismantled labs and in the radar building. There was also Al Bielek's half-brother, Duncan Cameron, who is a great psychic with the most extraordinary capabilities in mind control known to mankind. As part of the Philadelphia Experiment, Duncan—by using his extraordinary psychic powers—not only created physical manifestations, but was able to transport solid objects to distant locations. He even materialized a 25 foot tall monster that couldn't be stopped once created, eventually destroying numerous structures throughout the area."

Duncan Cameron, Preston Nichols, and Al Bielek, deep in underground Montauk.

Literally dumfounded, Helga soon uncovered Al Bielek's role in what went on in Montauk. "After traveling across time and space, Al was assigned to work with a 75 million dollar computer that had the incredible capability to tell what a person was thinking. The computer could also take human thoughts and use them at any given time without any further human input, simply by the operator pressing a button."

Armed with cameras, flashlights, and their guardian angels, Helga and companions entered the now partly-demolished (on purpose?) remains of the Montauk Army Base that to them quickly became "a grim reminder of a bygone era when human guinea pigs were used for psychic experiments to send men through time, and thought control was used to render them listless in what was evidently made into a underground 'chamber of horrors.'"

As Helga walked through the damp darkness, she was reminded of the Jews who had survived the holocaust of World

War II, and promised to tell the world that such atrocities would "never happen again."

"As I looked around me and thought of all the terrible things that had happened, I couldn't help but say a prayer to all those unsung heroes who were caught up in these ungodly experiments that displaced them in time.

"Duncan was not only one of the victims of the Philadelphia Experiment—along with Al Bielek—but he was also a survivor who somehow was not destroyed. To this day, he still struggles to cling to reality. His programming has allowed his boyish features to mask his innermost pain and suffering. Sometimes he clings to reality and then sometimes he has these mood swings that turn him into an almost militaristic, almost mechanical android in his mannerisms."

Helga asserts that such "personality shifts" are to be expected when you come to realize "what Duncan was subjected to by these so-called scientists," who were really more monsters than man. "He was," Helga states, "strapped in the nude, forced into a sexual high and just before ejaculation was bombarded with electrodes and probes similar to the 'shock treatment' given in order to satisfy this insane military mission."

Right in front of those present, Duncan broke down and began to sob. "I'm sorry. I'm sorry, please forgive me!" Helga and all the others wrapped their arms around Duncan to comfort him and to drive the "demons" from his mind and body.

According to the current tourist brochures, Montauk, Long Island is supposed to be a pleasant little town with magnificent ocean views, surfing, horseback riding, golf, tennis and salt water fishing. "Indeed," notes Helga, "there are gorgeous beaches, beautiful parks and historic sights to greet you as well as some of the best seafood restaurants and quaint nautical gift shops."

But there is something else here that is not so quaint.

"For this unassuming little town also has an abandoned military base complete with official signs warning people to—'KEEP OUT!'"

To the average person, this military base "is built to look like a real, lived-in town. There is even a neighborhood atmos-

A view of the old computer center in Montauk.

phere about the place. The base contains concrete buildings that would easily pass for regular family style dwellings. From the air—indeed—there would appear to be nothing out of the norm."

From what Helga tells us, the base was "officially recognized and utilized as part of the Eastern Shield radar defense in the fifties and sixties. It was also the place where horrors, equal to those inside a concentration camp, took place.

"Known as *Fort Hero* (Yes! there were many unsung heroes there), this three-tiered underground site was built prior to World War II. A fourth level is believed to have been deliberately flooded out to deter intruders. Oddly enough, recent evidence points to fifth and sixth levels that may still be active today.

"Along with Al Bielek, Preston Nichols and Duncan Cameron, I climbed into the bowels of Montauk and have personally seen and videotaped everything I am telling you so there can be no denial of what transpired at Montauk."

According to those directly involved, a great deal of Top Secret work involving time travel and preparations for the Philadelphia Experiment took place underground here with the help of many of our greatest scientific minds. And what might have started out as a simple experiment quickly took turns for the worse, to become one of the most perverted projects in human history.

Utilizing her keen observation, super psychic abilities, and sensitivity, Helga Morrow was especially aware of the unusual and eerie circumstances they were operating under at all times.

"Looking back, it looks mighty strange that the Montauk lighthouse was active with flying seagulls when we arrived, and that many large cats appearing to be about 15 pounds were sitting around the picnic area waiting for handouts. But shortly thereafter, there were no other signs of real life to be observed. There were no birds, squirrels, or the usual signs of activity one normally finds, once we entered the base area."

Helga says she also noticed something mighty peculiar about the townsfolk.

"When I walked down the street in the village where the shops and restaurants are, I noted many young men in their 20s and 30s all with blond hair and blue eyes. What made this so unusual is that everyone in the pizza shop sitting at the tables— as well as the waiters—almost all of them appeared identical (except for maybe an occasional mustache). It was the same in the fast food and carry-out stores. I couldn't help but think of the film, *The Boys From Brazil.*"

Even the conversation of those around them seemed unusual.

"I must have heard the words 'military base' whispered a thousand times. The eeriness soon crept in all around us. I felt as if the Montauk vacation area was a cover-up for some weird experiment that either went wrong, or was going to take place in the near future.

"Occasionally a black helicopter flew over us, but I guess my angels were working overtime, for we were not bothered, and I know if we had been spotted there would have been definite repercussions.

The ever-brave Helga Morrow, standing deep in the bowels of underground Montauk.

"Active radar emissions were sporadically picked up by our video camera. We became very much aware of interference, though we never did find out where it actually was emanating from. But something definitely was trying to interfere with the video reception.

"We wandered throughout the underground complex, but my most profound experience was when we reached the area where the young men used in demented sexual-psychic experiments were kept in cages. With my psychic vision, I could see the young men, all naked, lined up, waiting to be experimented upon. I could feel their anguish, their confusion! It was so painful I burst into tears just before Duncan broke into hysterical crying at what he had had to endure in this chamber of horrors.

"To relive this experience with Duncan, as a psychic and a minister, was, to say the least, devastating! As I write this, tears well in my eyes and my hands begin to shake. "What madness was this?' Why in the name of God—in a country that states on its dollar bill, 'In God We Trust'—does a thing of this nature occur? Why was this experiment not at least conducted in a humane fashion if that was at all possible? Why weren't these men ever de-programmed humanely? They were simply cast aside as if they were 'used' merchandise.

"By using 425–450 Mhz radio frequency power, the human mind can be manipulated and controlled. By changing the pulse, you can be made to laugh, cry, show anger, fear, whatever is wanted. As recently as Vietnam, various frequencies were hurled at the Viet Cong that were so strong that they shattered the ear drums of the people, bursting in their heads and of course killing them.

"Sexual submissiveness is nothing new. It is the primary Kundalini force that made these experiments work! By hooking up the Cray 1 and the IBM computers to the subjects, Duncan in this case was capable of creating the Montauk Monster from his own mind. The monster not only became a reality, but this beast broke up a building as if it were an erector set. This incident was filmed as proof!"

This sort of bizarre experimentation is very much reminiscent of the "Monster from the Id" creature in the classic 1950's science-fiction film, *Forbidden Planet*. In that flick, a scientist has his mind altered by a powerful, alien computer and his subconscious creates a huge, invincible monster to seek revenge against his supposed "enemies." One wonders just how the scientists who designed the Montauk experiments—possibly with the best of intentions, and oblivious to the dire consequences—might have been influenced by this film.

"The 25-foot beast developed a mind of its own and kept destroying everything in its path. Eventually the powers that helped create the Montauk Monster panicked and began unplugging the machines in the hope of stopping its madness. They had no such luck! It continued its mayhem. Preston Nichols remembers torching the equipment and some of the scientists taking axes to the machinery. We photographed the torch marks and the other evident devastation to the equipment. Major funding had to be acquired for this madness

A view from the outside of the old computer center in Montauk.

and experts have informed me that Nazi gold bullion was behind it."

Furthermore, Helga reveals that her main reason "in going to Montauk was because I had learned that my father, Dr. Fred A. Kueppers, had worked there as a scientist during World War II. When my family and I were told that he had passed away in 1962, I spent the next 30 years in pursuit of the truth, and only by the grace of God found it. Preston Nichols knew my father and remembered with great affection details of my father's work as one of the key figures in the Montauk time experiments.

"As time went on, lengthy questions about my father were answered by Preston, including the fact that he had only worked on Time Experiments and none of the horrible experiments that Duncan had unfortunately been involved with.

"Preston informed me that father was quite a humanitarian, scholar, scientist and very well liked by his co-workers who affectionately referred to him as Fred or Koop. I have photographs that corroborate earlier stories and confirm Preston's as well.

"Preston is an erudite, jolly individual with more information at his disposal than can be found in most encyclopedias. He is a pleasure to talk with, a great teacher, scientist and inventor and is also Duncan's best friend. Together they are business partners in Space-Time Labs, a fully equipped manufacturer of psychic-active electronic equipment.

Preston invited me to his lab that was a mixture of Tesla, von Neuman, Einstein and Montauk. The mind boggles, since I know little of this machinery or its workings. However, I returned home with a great deal of hands-on knowledge.

"I have learned a few unerring facts directly from Preston, and Al Bielek. One being that molecular objects do not break down in a few days, but in fact they break down in minutes! Matter does not turn to dust, dust 'is' matter (objects, buildings, etc.). The Montauk beast never turned to dust, but was sent into hyperspace to another time.

"Since it was created, it could not be destroyed, only removed to another reality/another dimension to get 'it' out of the way. Conversely, if someone were to plug into that very dimension or reality, the object/person/beast, etc., would ultimately return to its full function and original purpose. Figuratively speaking, the Montauk beast could be set down in the middle of Times Square and wreak havoc if the correct electronic equipment were used.

"These days, computers and modern technology have become so miniaturized and improved that the colossal machinery and cumbersome equipment of the original Montauk and Philadelphia Experiments is but a pile of scrap metal and history to what was once the finest equipment on earth."

Helga claims that due to what came out of the Montauk and Philadelphia Experiments, the mechanism necessary to send an animal, person or thing into another time or dimension can now fit into an ordinary briefcase. "The technique is less dangerous and painful and most important the intact return is not painful nor is the risk of reversing the molecules prevalent, such as returning in the 'mirror image' of oneself.

What is new wiring doing in an "abandoned" underground base in Montauk?

"When Al Bielek was sent forward into time," notes Helga, "this procedure took roughly 20 minutes. The young recruits, Al and others, who were sent forward in time were to report what they experienced. There was a golden horse with mysterious inscriptions on it that was surrounded by buildings that had been destroyed. These men (subjects, including Al) were specifically trained to stay inside of a 20 foot diameter area or they were told they would not return. Those who disobeyed did not return. Not because they didn't want to, but because they could not!

"Being lost in space was not deliberate nor treated lightly among scientists. Unfortunately, many were lost in time for all eternity. But those like Al can describe their experiences with total accuracy."

According to Helga, she saw and touched the old Thyratron tube "that was used to bend time. With the Ampletron nearby, I photographed both for my records and for a film now being edited.

"While wandering around the bowels of Montauk, I was particularly fascinated by a huge glass and crystal tube, over five feet tall, with circular crystals inside. It looks exactly like the vertical glass chambers from the *Star Trek* program that are used to beam people up.

"I don't pretend to know everything we have learned from the Philadelphia Experiment, and I dare say you need a crash course in Quantum Physics to understand the workings of all I have witnessed. Consequently, travelling on a beam of light is over simplified. If you are at point 'A,' 'B' remains over here. To get from point 'A' to point 'B' is linear. However, if you FOLD the paper like a rubber band, aligning 'A' to 'B' then point 'A' would snap to point 'B' and 'B' would go back to its natural place in hyperspace. Point 'A' would then become point 'Bs' reality.

"Reversing the procedure would bring it back (in theory). This is not done on a beam of light, but with the scrambled molecules on a special frequency sent AT THE SPEED OF LIGHT to the point of reference.

"Returning sometimes causes a 'mirror image' reverse distortion, such as in the movie *The Fly*, until this process has been perfected. Sometimes the organs or partial organs remain outside the body. Eventually, these links were worked out. Therefore when my father appeared to me in full third dimensional form, he was in pain to remain with me till he returned to his 'alternate reality' in hyperspace. Fortunately, this process was improved on mechanically; however, the theory has not changed."

While in Montauk, Helga was invited to speak at Preston Nichols and Peter Moon's "Montauk Night," at which about 30 people attended.

"My overall view of Montauk was the first impression of the Montauk lighthouse, the tourist shops, and the visitor's center that camouflaged the deeper meaning of Montauk. The deeper meaning is the legacy Montauk has hidden from the public and is only spoken of in whispers."

As far as Helga is concerned, "They can either tear down

the base and deny it exists, or clean it up and make it an histor-
ical part for all to see. But why leave it as an eyesore, a military
blight? In my opinion, certain facts have to be brought out.
This is why I have tried to document this information. This is
clearly the truth about Montauk and how it effects each of our
lives—Al, Preston, Duncan and myself. Each of us had our own
story to tell and, hopefully, the next book about Montauk and
my own video will hit upon a nerve of reality! All is not the way
it seems. REALITY is all in the hands of the few who control it!"

Putting two and two together, it is very apparent that there
is still much in the way of unseen energies operating in and
around Montauk. Helga Morrow promises she will look into the
matter more fully as time goes on, while our friend and Philadelphia Experiment survivor, Al Bielek, tries to call upon even
more memories of all that went on in his life following the teleportation of the USS *Eldridge* into another dimension and time
frame.

If this talk of underground laboratories, weird acts of sexual perversion and creation of a 25 foot tall monster are even
half true, our government has an awful lot of explaining to do.
From what we now know, the Philadelphia Experiment and
Montauk Project would easily pale the Watergate cover-up and
the Contra affair, having a disastrous effect on our nation's
economy and political stability. But I have always believed the
truth must prevail and so it will in this instance as well as it has
many times in the history of our great nation.

• • •

Please Note: Those wishing to contact Helga Morrow about
her Montauk video or her work as a psychic may write her
directly at 3661 North Campbell (#370), Tucson, AZ 85719. Be
sure to include a stamped, self-addressed envelope for a personal reply.

Chapter Eight
The Philadelphia
Experiment: An Update
—The Correspondence

While it may be a surprise to a lot of folks, apparently there are any number out there who know more about the Philadelphia Experiment than we give them credit for.

Up until he passed away just a couple of years ago, Carlos Allende was still running around talking about what happened to those on the *Eldridge*, though, in general, it seems that people thought him "quite mad" to the point where he would babble almost incoherently. He did meet with Gray Barker a couple of times. The late researcher tried to pump Allende for more information on the ill-fated experiment, but could get little more out of him than had already been reported.

Barker did, however, receive regular correspondence from those who claimed to have the "inside word" on what had transpired back in 1943. Here is a sample of the letters he received:

• • •

Dear Mr. Barker,

My name is Douglas Earl Rushford. I have done a lot of reading on Dr. Jessup, which recalls an incident while I was in Philadelphia.

I got robbed and had to get something to eat. I ran into some boys and started talking to one of them. He said," Come on with me." Well, after listening to about an hour of some guy telling me that God loves you and all this, me and the three other guys got one slice of bread and a bowl of onion soup. I stayed there that night and me and this guy started talking about space ships, and he says, "Shoot, that ain't nothing," and then he told me how, when he was in the Navy back in 1941, him and some guys took part in what's called thin air, and that's why he's a bum today. That after the Navy saw that it was doing things to the men, they just discharged him as a mental case. My friend died in his sleep that night.

Mr. Barker, I would like you to tell me everything you know about this thin air and the documents that you have. I feel I should try in every way to bring this to the people. I think that man wants me to do that and he knew I would and now he can rest. I'll stay in touch and what I learn I'll forward it to you.

Forever yours,
D.E. Rushford

• • •

Dear Mr. Barker,

While attending a Navy electronics school in 1976, I heard a very interesting but vague account of an experiment in which a Navy ship and its crew were said to have become invisible. We were studying magnetics at the time. The instructor said the experiment involved creating a strong magnetic field about the ship, but he knew little else about the project.

I dismissed this account as just another BS story told to pass the time on a slow day. It wasn't until about a month ago when a friend and I were discussing the possible use of levitation or antigravity to move the huge stones of Coral Castle in Florida that I again heard of this experiment. My friend turned me on to the book *The Philadelphia Experiment* by W.L. Moore. Very well researched and written.

Anyway, I got your address from this book and understand I can obtain a facsimile copy of the *Varo Annotated Edition* of Jessup's *The Case for the UFO* from you. Can I still get a copy of this book or any other information on this subject? Any help will be appreciated by the both of us.

Sincerely,
Steve Cummings

• • •

Dear Mr. Barker,

I have been interested in unexplained phenomena for a very long time. But what intrigues me most of all is the notorious Philadelphia Experiment.

I live in the vicinity of the Philadelphia Naval Base and the alleged occurrence has emerged as something of a local legend here, and is a topic of intense debate. I have inquired among many South Philadelphians about this enigma, and those who can recall it emphasize wholeheartedly its validity. However, my parents, Basil and Edith Merenda, cannot recall it, even though my father was a Naval veteran of World War II and both of my parents had business in the area around the Naval base at that time.

But they do remember the then existing taverns frequented by sailors, where the "ruckus" described by Allende and the Moore/Berlitz book may have taken place. The favorite watering hole of the Philadelphia seamen was the "Big House," which is no longer in existence. It was located at Broad Street and Oregon Avenue.

Sincerely,
Joseph J. Merenda

• • •

Dear Gray,

Many researchers feel that Dr. Jessup's death (supposedly by suicide) ties in with the Philadelphia Experiment, and of course the book by that title has added to this mystery and created a great deal of controversy in general. Of course, some skeptics yell for more proof.

In a recent interview, co-author William Moore said that a great deal has happened since the book was written and that the additional evidence makes him even more convinced that there is something to this enigma.

"Shortly after the book came out," he said, "I was actually

contacted by a man who says he was a member of the crew of the *Eldridge*. After corresponding we met, and this man had an envelope full of documents to prove his story. He said he had remained in the Navy until 1960 when he retired as a commander. According to Moore, the commander claimed to have been put in a hospital for six months after the experiment, having been told by the Navy that he was suffering from a "nervous breakdown."

As part of the documentation he had to offer, the man gave Moore the names of two men who were involved in the incident. One name led Moore to the son of one of those individuals.

"The man told him his father had been killed in what the Navy described as an 'accident' in 1953!" In July, 1980, Moore was approached by a fellow writer who had been reading through *The Philadelphia Experiment* on a bus. According to Moore's assistant, he was traveling alone when another passenger took a seat beside him and said he knew all about the incident, that one of his friends had been on the USS *Eldridge* when it became invisible.

"I have found out that the man lives in California and that it is quite interesting, since my commander friend has told me the only other survivor of the *Eldridge* lived in that state."

Moore also received a letter from a man who said that, during 1950, he had seen a film made for people in top security defense work. "He described what sounds like the Philadelphia Experiment being shown at the beginning of a black and white film sequence," Moore noted.

I am excited about the new book, *The Jessup Dimension*, you are publishing, after reading the manuscript chapter you sent to me. I'm certain it is going to throw more light onto the Jessup/Allende affair!

Kind regards,
Timothy Green Beckley
Editor, *UFO Review*

• • •

Back in the 1960s, researcher and best-selling author Brad

Steiger began writing about the Philadelphia Experiment in earnest. In fact, Brad is the only individual to have put together a mass-market magazine—a "one shot" special—that sold over a hundred thousand copies at newsstands nationwide. *The Allende Letters* did a good job of reviewing what was known about the Philadelphia Experiment at the time, which, naturally, isn't anything like the information we are able to assemble today.

Over the years, Steiger has kept on top of matters pertaining to the Philadelphia Experiment. In fact, giving credit where credit is due, it was Brad who actually "discovered" Al Bielek at a barbecue given by his typesetter while living in Phoenix, Arizona. Bielek enthralled Steiger with his knowledge of the Philadelphia Experiment to the point where it was hard to believe that Bielek didn't have some sort of working knowledge of what had taken place. In turn, Steiger introduced Al Bielek to publisher Timothy Green Beckley, who invited the six-footer to speak at his annual National New Age and Alien Agenda Conference, which is held each September in Phoenix. Beckley was impressed by what he saw and heard (at one point he said the outside hallway was packed with people trying to learn more from Bielek, even after his talk was officially over).

If you want to read more about the Philadelphia Experiment and Al Bielek, you'll want to get Brad Steiger's impressive work, *The Philadelphia Experiment and Other UFO Conspiracies,* available for $15.00 from Inner Light, Box 753, New Brunswick, NJ 08903. Just like in the case of Gray Barker, writer Steiger has found his mailbox from time to time full of correspondence related to this mystery. Here are excerpts from just a few of the letters he's filed away.

• • •

One letter implied that the writer had been a seaman aboard the vessel on which the alleged experiment had taken place. "You would not write of this so objectively if you were forced to live with this horror," the man wrote.

Several correspondents told of being harassed by ominous and effective "agents" after they had promised to reveal more.

One letter stated that the correspondent could "tell things that would make everything clear." A follow-up letter from me produced the reply: "They found out. They won't let me talk."

Another letter began: "Your work is so accurate that you scare me....Your writings seek to explain the mysteries of the world in a 'scientific way.' I wish that I could tell you more, but we who are controlled could upset *their* whole system if we would speak. Therefore, these *people* who direct us make certain that we do not speak! Study your own writings, and you may discover the *real* truth!"

An anonymous writer told of witnessing phenomena which he believed to be related to the alleged secret Navy experiment. During the Second World War, his landlady's son went into the Navy, and it was believed he had died while in service. Some years later, however, our correspondent met a young man of the son's description in the hallway of the rooming house. The young man said "hello," then "vanished like a ghost."

The boarder often saw the young man appear, then vanish. On one occasion, the strange man appeared, began to weep, and begged the landlady for some bread. The matter became even more confused in the boarder's mind when the young sailor's widow, who continued to reside with her mother-in-law for many years after her husband's presumed death, moved out after obtaining a *divorce*.

Had the landlady's son been one of those unfortunate seamen aboard the experimental naval vessel? Was he even now, years later, still lapsing into invisibility and suffering the torments of the damned? Such questions have plagued our anonymous correspondent for many years.

Chapter Nine
Has Dr. Jessup
Communicated From
The "Other Side"?

Besides his interest in the Philadelphia Experiment and UFOs, Jessup also held a fascination with the possibility of life after death. Though he did not declare himself a spiritualist while still alive, he did some minor research in the area of parapsychology. Interestingly enough, following his "suicide" at least one medium purported to have heard from Morris who felt inclined to let his voice be heard from the "other side."

Normally, the medium in question would go into a trance and an entity would come through. On this particular occasion, however, there was a lot more involved. "I felt as if my vocal cords and mouth and tongue movements were being seized by a powerful force and made to form and utter the words."

According to those attending the sitting, this seance seemed more "intense than others."

The medium noted that the spirit coming through his vocal cords did not identify himself as to his name but mentioned that he was involved in UFO research while on the Earthly plane.

Proclaimed the spirit:

"I was well known for my work in this field. And I do think I have a few of the answers now that I did not have before. I cannot answer many of the questions I proposed in my writings on this subject, for this was on a, well, what you would call a physical level, as you would understand it. I was concerned whether the objects were coming from some other planet in the usual sense you would think of. Let me say in the same way you would consider your building a rocket ship and taking off for and landing on Mars. This all may well be true, though before I came here I was beginning to believe we were not having any such physical visitations. Let me say the visitations you are having are nevertheless no less real. I am on that particular plane right now and everything is very real around me. I have been transported in the saucers and I know they are solid. When you crack your shin bone on a railing you know they are solid."

The questioning then got around to the manner in which the speaker had expired. The answer came from the spirit cinched the fact that it was Jessup talking.

• • •

Q: When did you die?

A: There is some question in my mind if I really died. Because I was there one moment and somewhere else the next. I could still see my body and it was very much alive. They made it appear as if I were dead. I think I died sometime afterward, but there are more important things to discuss, for I have limited time.

Q: If you didn't die, there is a lot to straighten out. If you could tell us where you were when you died or whatever happened to you, maybe we could understand what really happened and inform you about it. We have helped many people who are on other planes and don't understand what has happened.

A: I am told that to get my message best understood I should not dwell on subjects such as this. Some mysteries remain mysteries for now. Anyhow, this does not seem to be very important. Do not think of me as an omnipotent genius who knows everything. On Earth I had an IQ of around 150 and that's what I have here—but of course we do not have that kind of test here.

I saw my body before it had died and I saw its discovery.

That is all I can remember. I was in a craft, a flying saucer if you please, and I was flying away from the city in which I had lived. Gradually the view of the city faded, as if I were changing existence, and I found myself apparently in space. A great window encircled the entire interior. This circular window varied from translucent to complete transparency, though interspersed in the window were small circles of varying transparency. The window was about five feet in height. The window then gradually faded to an entire translucence, and finally to opacity. The small circles remained translucent or transparent, though constantly changing. I guessed these might represent the traditional port holes which saucer sighters have reported.

Q: Who was piloting the craft?

A: A man, obviously a normal earth man, dressed, as I remember so clearly, in a T-Shirt and gray work trousers. This man did not tell me who he was, but immediately called me by my first name and assured me that no harm would come to me, that he was only following orders which would be for my own good as well as for the good of all mankind. This man refused to tell me where we were going, but asked me several questions about what I had been doing and what had been going on in the world. He gave me the impression of one who had been away from Earth a great while. The craft apparently ran on an automatic pilot system, for although he sat before controls, in a large swivel chair, he paid little attention to these controls, and kept his chair turned toward me, where I was sitting on a ledge that encircled the interior at the base of the window.

Trip to Venus

Soon the window became transparent and I discovered a change had taken place in the outside scene. While I previously had the impression of travelling in space, it now appeared that we were flying through clouds or vapor, and it was very much like being on an airliner while climbing or descending through clouds. In fact, I remember feeling slight bumps as one experiences when an airliner hits turbulence, though this was very slight.

A most beautiful country then met my view. This would be

impossible to describe, even though I had more time to do so. Our descent was so rapid that I got very little view of it anyhow at that time, and we landed. We landed in a courtyard connected with a very large building, which I can best describe as being made of metallic glass, the same varying translucence as in the window being present.

I was met by three people about six feet in height, very beautiful people, all male, dressed in an odd costume of spun glass-like appearance. Nothing like a ski suit, I might add, having read of such Earth contacts, but more like a uniform. These people smiled, called me by name and told me to come with them.

I was taken into a large conference type of room and seated very comfortably. Shorter people, not as beautiful, and of a distinct negroid or mongoloid appearance (though their skins were very white), entered bearing several trays containing food and drink. I will not dwell on this, except to give you some of the details you mentally ask. The food was not recognizable, but tasted similar to food I was used to, though it could not be identified exactly as to state. The food at that time was mainly in briquette form, as if it were processed food. A large melon was served which tasted similar, but not exactly like watermelon or other kinds of melon I had known. The food was not the most delicious I had ever eaten, but I discovered that I was very hungry and devoured all of it. The drink I was served was a blue liquid with an obvious fruit juice base, but with some fermentation and an effect not unlike what a slight alcoholic content would cause.

These three individuals sat with me as I ate and informed me I was chosen for a definite role which I could assume if I so desired. I was told that I could not return to where I had come from because my body was now dead. If I did not care for the work which they had selected, I could choose some other type of work, or do nothing and go on living there, which I was then told was Venus. If I cared to carry out the work, which would be most difficult, great spiritual rewards would accrue to me. This occupation, I was told, involved work with human beings on Earth.

Some of this work I do not yet fully understand. Minor work in which I have been engaged has consisted of mental contact with an Earth scientist, who does not realize such contact exists. This scientist has written a book, a very good book, and I believe part of its merits are due to my guidance. I was not able to get through to the collaborator of this book, however.

I am still going to school, so to speak, and will for quite some time. This education involves philosophy of sorts, which I believe to be the type of re-education all earth people must have if they are to avoid consequences of a catastrophic nature.

Along with my schooling I have had a great deal of pleasure in visiting my adopted planet and learning something of the ways of living there and of the technology there.

Q: Where are you now?

A: This is a difficult concept for me to understand or to communicate to you, for I do not believe the frame of reference would be the same. This is not some kind of fourth dimension, which I still believe to represent time, but a state of existence very close to yours, but only slightly removed from your physical existence. I believe that when the philosophies of earth people are changed, the mere difference in thinking will tend to connect this world and yours on a plane of reality. Remember what I said about my IQ. It is still 150. I am still a poor card player—yes I'm afraid I introduced the game to some of my colleagues—and I still could not fix a vacuum sweeper in your home if it went bad.

Attending School

Q: What do you and the people you are with believe about God and religion?

A: I am still attending school, so to speak, and can yet see only glimmerings of the realities involving deity, which I would prefer to call it. Let me say that from the knowledge which has been imparted to me I would say that man's greatest sacrilege is the practice of creating God in his own image, and that this anthropomorphism is not only ridiculous, it is as sinful as cheating your neighbor, or maybe even more so. I do not understand what or who God is, for you cannot find it by seeking this ultimate image. You will find more of an approach to deity in your every-day living than you will in abstract contemplation or going to church.

Before I go let me note that the best way to approach my present world involves the lessening involvement with your own physical world. This is a very practical matter and is easily begun. Reduced to very simplified language, let me say that you cannot fly to Venus overnight, but you can begin to note what you would term "spiritual values" more than you would note "physical values," (quotation marks that of the editor) such as occupation with automobiles, fine homes, preoccupation with physical sex, and so on. Once you get away from the physical involvements with your world mentally, you will find that it gradually melts away and you are in an entirely different environment. The world you are seeking is that of an intense "spiritual" one recaptured physically on the next higher plane, but I don't believe I have expressed this concept very clearly.

Anyhow, if this represents oversimplification, it is on the right track. Have you ever been driving along in your car, and voluntarily given some other driver the right of way, such as helping him out into the lane of traffic, for example, when other cars behind you would likely not do so? This represents a slightly less involvement with your own physical world. Did you notice how the sun shone more brightly, how the scenery, if even momentarily, became more beautiful? To a very slight degree, your physical world changed. Think how much would have changed had you emphasized your lack of physical involvement to a greater degree. I want to caution you not to go hogwild into such an attempted development, without the proper guidance. Remember that the words I have spoken represent an oversimplification.

UFOs in the Sky

Q: Are the saucers such as you traveled to Venus in still visiting us?

A: These visits have been going on for centuries, and will continue. They have not been too meaningful until recently. These are not necessarily exploratory craft. Due to an increase in the awareness of human beings, who, despite what you may hear and think, are nevertheless rising in consciousness, these craft are seen more than previously. I think you realize, though, that not everybody sees these saucers. Have you noticed that most people who tell you of seeing saucers are people who, if you think about it, seem to have a greater awareness than the average individual? In fact, usually they are spoken of, in the press, and by their neighbors, as people who have a great reputation for truth, and are extremely well thought of. If you think about this you may be able to deduce a part of what I am saying about a general increase in awareness.

Yet these saucers are not seen generally. I do not think, for example, that the President of the United States sees them or is aware of them. You will find that there is indeed something unique involved between the people who see the saucers and those who do not see the saucers. I never saw what I could distinguish as a saucer without doubt while I was on Earth, though I constantly searched the skies for them.

Q: Why are you on this plane, then, with obviously increased awareness and a higher level of consciousness, if you did not have this before and could not see the saucers before?

A: This I do not attempt to understand and I believe I am where I am because of some technology developed by the Venusians.

Q: Do you think the Earth is going to be destroyed by atomic bombs?

A: I have asked about this, but my teachers either do not know or will not tell me. They do not seem to be gravely concerned about the matter. It is my impression that they believe they can prevent this, either by some means of their own which are technical, or by the education of Earth man.

Q: Are the saucers going to land at any time and reveal themselves (This and previous questions not otherwise noted were asked vocally).

A: That depends upon what kind of saucers you are referring to. As an intelligent man who knows something of the universe on a plane of Earth level, I believe that the Earth has been visited many times in the past by intelligent beings of your level, and that the Earth may be visited again. I do not believe the people of my present existence will make such a landing, or whether they could if they wanted to at this time. Anyhow, I am not permitted to reveal everything and information of this nature must be imparted gradually. Let this information be known to UFO circles if they are interested in hearing it. I must go now, and I thank you for listening.

• • •

The control of the medium vanished as soon as it began. The regular seance was not held because of the excitement caused by the extraordinary communication. The medium remembered most everything that was transmitted, as opposed to lack of memory in usual trance states.

Not having been there when the seance took place, we cannot say with a hundred percent certainty that it was really Dr. M. K. Jessup coming through the medium. Nonetheless from the message given from the spirit entity it would seem highly likely that this was actually the case.

But was Jessup actually speaking to us from the other side?

With what we now know regarding the intricacies involving the Philadelphia Experiment, it might have been that his death was really staged and that a dummy was buried in his place (several of those who reportedly saw Jessup after his passing claimed that they did not recognize his corpse). Much like Al Bielek, its possible that Jessup was invited to get more personally involved with the Philadelphia Experiment. He could have been invited to go on a mission into the future with the technology that had been invented. Or he could have gone dimension hopping, and he might have been speaking from some other realm much like Dr. Kueppers is said to have materialized in front of his daughter.

In closing we can easily say that the Philadelphia Experiment is not yet a "closed book." We have more than likely not heard the last from Al Bielek, and possibly not even from Dr. Jessup. Though the 1943 teleportation of the *Eldridge* is now a page out of history, when you consider that those involved found themselves traveling around from time frame to time frame, its possible that this vessel could even "show up" somewhere else to haunt those who are still trying to keep the Philadelphia Experiment a closely guarded secret.

Time will tell...or will time hold yet another secret?

We will just have to wait and see!

Appendix I
Navy Has Its "Tricks" To Make Carriers Disappear

Editor's Note: Lest you begin to think that the Navy has never commented on its own attempts to make its vessels invisible to the enemy, a news story appeared in countless papers across America back in August of 1986, describing what are "officially" termed "blackout conditions." The story speaks quite well for itself and ran as follows:

• • •

Navy has lots of tricks to make carriers disappear

WASHINGTON, D.C. (AP)—U.S. Navy aircraft carriers, despite their incredible size, are becoming adept at a form of magic.

Utilizing weather, speed, advanced logistical planning and high-tech tomfoolery, several carriers in recent months have managed to vanish from antagonists' eyes into the vastness of the oceans, reappearing only at the moment of attack.

Last April, dogged by airplanes rented by American television networks and by Soviet intelligence vessels, the carriers *Coral Sea* and *America* dropped from sight off the coast of Sicily. Less than 24 hours later, their planes bombed targets in Libya.

And just over a month ago, a much lengthier case of a

"missing" carrier occurred during an exercise named RIMPAC 86. The USS *Ranger,* although the target of an intense search that included satellite reconnaissance, escaped detection for two weeks while sailing across the Pacific.

The performance was considered all the more remarkable by an Australian admiral who monitored the exercise, because the carrier's planes were flying sorties throughout the period, staging mock attacks against surface ships, submarines and land targets.

Rear Adm. I.W. Knox of the Royal Australian Navy disclosed recently the "Orange" forces in RIMPAC could not locate the Ranger "from the time it departed Southern Californian exercise areas until it steamed into Pearl Harbor some 14 days later."

Reports of such exploits delight Navy brass, who must answer critics who think carriers are sitting ducks in an age of nuclear-powered submarines and cruise missiles.

Modern-day carriers have yet to be tested in combat against Soviet weaponry. But they are practicing hard at what the Navy calls "maneuver strategy"—if the enemy can't find you, you have surprise. And with surprise, you can win.

Navy spokesmen decline to discuss war-fighting tactics, citing military secrecy. But several officers interviewed recently who asked not to be identified, say the idea of a "stealthy carrier" is not so far-fetched.

Consider:

• The *Coral Sea* and *America* accomplished their feats through a variety of tricks, but the most important were "masking" and "EMCON." The details of masking are classified, but essentially it involves making another ship—a destroyer, for example—look and sound like a car and a carrier look like something else.

The process normally begins when a carrier is under radar surveillance, but beyond visual sight. The decoy ship maintains the carrier's previous course, while the carrier speeds away.

"We can make the Soviets believe another ship is the carrier," says one official. "The radar image, broadcasting pilot talk and the radio sounds of flight operations, the lighting at night:

It looks like a duck and sounds like a duck so it must be a duck. So they follow the duck and make a mistake."

The carrier, meantime, can employ lighting at night that makes it look like a tanker.

• Also employed by the Coral Sea and America, and the key to the *Ranger's* disappearing act, was EMCON. This is the equivalent of a submarine "rigging for silence" or a convoy traveling under blackout conditions.

EMCON is a Navy acronym for emission control. Emission, in this case, refers to the electronic signals that are radiated by such equipment as radar, sonar and radio. When a carrier goes to EMCON, it literally shuts down much of its electronic gear to avoid detection.

Navy officials say a carrier can operate for long periods in EMCON because "we go mute, but not deaf or blind."

The procedure works by utilizing E2-C Hawkeye radar planes, flying at some distance from the carrier. Everything the Hawkeye sees is relayed electronically to the carrier and its escorts, providing a picture of aerial activity as well as surface forces.

While transmitting, the Hawkeye is far from the carrier, which gets the plane's signals passively without any transmission of its own. The Hawkeye also takes on the role of air-traffic controller for the carrier's planes.

Replenishment tankers, meantime, are told well in advance to make their own way to a specific position in the ocean. Again, radio silence is maintained.

• Aviation tactics. Even if radar can't pick up a carrier sailing beyond the horizon, the ship's location can be betrayed by jet aircraft scrambling into the air. The Navy's answer is called "offset vector."

"To be simplistic, the planes don't climb," says one officer. "They catapult off and literally hit the deck. If planes are suddenly popping up 100 miles from the ship, you have no idea where they came from."

• Speed. Publicly, the Navy says its carriers are capable of speeds "in excess of 30 knots." Privately, officers acknowledge the floating cities can approach 40 knots.

"We can literally outrun the Soviet tattletales (intelligence ships)," says one. "And in (heavy) weather of any kind, there's no contest. The carrier can outrun its own escorts."

• Weather and Satellites. Anyone who's been caught in the rain after the weatherman forecast sunny skies has his own thoughts on meteorology. But there have been solid gains made within that science in recent years.

"Although really heavy weather can hurt flight operations, these guys know how to follow weather patterns and use rain storms and above all, cloud cover," says one official. "The carriers can receive weather data via satellite, passively, without portraying their position."

"And we know the orbital parameters of Soviet reconnaissance satellites as well as our own," adds another. "If there's a recon bird coming by and you can duck into some weather, you duck into the weather. Or if you know there's a blind spot in coverage, you sail there."

"Once you succeed in slipping away," summarizes one officer. "the odds shift in your favor. Most people don't have any conception of how big the oceans are. You can be lonely if you want."

Appendix II
Confidential Report on
Secrets of Invisibility

Wouldn't it be nice to be able to disappear upon command?

Think of all the absolutely incredible things that you could do if you weren't visible to the human eye.

You could walk into a room undetected.

You could listen to others as they converse in private.

You'd be able to visit friends and foe alike without having them know that they were being "spied" upon.

You could visit the theater, the movies, a ball game and stand or sit anywhere you wanted—even back stage.

If you were dishonest, you could even walk into a bank and walk out with a sack full of money and the cash wouldn't be missed until you were safely home.

Throughout history—believe it or not—there have been those individuals who claim that they can make their flesh and bones "fade" from view. These master adepts use mystical, metaphysical or occult powers. They are advanced humans who have discovered various techniques that give them supernatural powers. Some of them have used magick, others have above average mental abilities. It's freaky, it's bizarre—but apparently it's possible to learn such techniques yourself. Some say the secret of invisibility can be learned relatively quickly. Others maintain that it takes years of study. Some say it happens by accident. Others profess that they can make themselves vanish upon command.

Moses—The Great Magician

Most of us think of Moses as being the mortal who was the closest to God. According to Biblical reference Moses actually spoke to the Lord. However, not many of us realize that Moses was a great seer. He was a mystic who understood and acted upon cosmic or universal laws. He was able to turn his staff into a snake when he was in danger and he could perform other amazing feats because he knew certain cosmic laws that were handed down to him by the Supreme Being.

Most Jewish historians say that Moses was murdered by ambitious politicians, but it may be that Moses simply faded away when the time came for him to vanish. In the book, *Antiquities of the Jews,* by Josephus, we read the following passage:

"As he went to the place where he was to vanish from their sight, they all followed after him weeping, but Moses beckoned with his hand to all who were remote from him, and told them to stay behind in quiet. All those who accompanied him were the senate, and Eleazar, the High Priest, and Joshua, their commander. As soon as they had come to the mountain called Abarim, Moses dismissed the senate, and a clone stood over him on the sudden, and he disappeared."

There are those that assume that Moses ascended into Heaven, just as Christ did. But there is some debate regarding this issue. H. Spencer Lewis, founder and first Imperator of the Rosicrucian Order, believed that the cloud referred to was a mystical cloud and that Jesus actually disappeared—possibly into another dimension—while on the ground.

Oliver Leroy, a noted authority on religion says that in his study of Catholic Saints, "It is possible to account for the vanishing of a levitated person...not by the incredible heights reached...in his ascent... but by the phenomenon of invisibility, some instances of which are to be found in the lives of several Saints."

Surrounded In a Cloud

There is something about a dark cloud that invokes

thoughts of mystery. Entire Armies have been known to disappear inside clouds. During World War I a troop of Australian soldiers marched down into a valley covered in mist and they were never seen again. We're not talking about two or three people here, but an entire troop. Such cases are well documented and can be found in many books and journals.

More recently a Canadian mystic, Richard Maurice Bucke, had the same kind of experience. He stated that without warning of any kind he found himself wrapped in a flame-colored cloud. For a moment he thought there was a great fire somewhere, but then he realized that the light was from within himself. He felt a sense of exultation, of joyousness, accompanied by an intellectual illumination quite impossible to describe. Bucke was so moved by this experience that he spent the rest of his life studying it. His special name for it was Cosmic Consciousness. Such self-illumination is part of the practice of invisibility according to many who have accomplished this seemingly remarkable feat, which may not be so remarkable once the principles of how it can be applied are fully understood.

Spiritualists Call It Ectoplasm

If you've ever read anything about the history of Spiritualism you'll know the importance of the substance called ectoplasm that flows from the mouths or other orifaces of mediums while in a trance. They use this ectoplasm to make a table levitate and sometimes this cotton candy-like substance can even form itself into an apparition. Researcher Charles Richet studied this phenomenon for many years. He was able to divide the formation of ectoplasm into three or four stages. The first stage included nothing invisible, but there were rappings. Objects were often moved about. Sitters felt that they were touched. The second stage revealed the formation of a cloud. This is just barely visible. When the cloud becomes more luminous, Richet called it the third stage. At this point, a human nude shape started to form. The fourth stage is one in which the complete human body is formed, or materialized. That shape that emerges from the ectoplasm does not have to be human. It can be an animal, or flowers, or even an inanimate object. Some say that before you can hope to become invisible you have to master the art of producing ectoplasm. But it can be done. All it takes is concentration, meditation and altering your consciousness.

The Seven Step Method

If you want to read a terrific book, you should try to obtain Steve Richards' *Invisibility* (Aquarian Publishing, England). Mr. Richards covers the topic from A to Z.

His seven step method is practiced widely and the only "equipment" you really need is a "laboratory," which, in this case, just happens to be a room with limited light coming in from the outside. One bare wall is also essential, or perhaps a door that leads into a darkened room. Most important of all is privacy. A skeptic in the room will insure failure.

Sit quietly and comfortably. You should then direct your gaze to one single area. This is important. The cloud will then form at the place that holds your attention. If you shift your gaze to other spots in the room, the cloud will not have a chance to build up. Your effort is cumulative. The longer you look at one area, the more definite the cloud becomes.

For best results, Richards suggests you de-focus your eyes. Look beyond what is in front of you, as if you are looking ten miles away. Some authorities suggest that you keep your eyes half open. With this idea you will have to experiment. Some experts say a cloud forms better against a black background rather than a white one. You will have to practice de-focusing your eyes. With a little concentration you can do it. Without it, the technique is useless.

Chanting is suggested, but you might find it distracting. Steve Richards does not do it for that reason. Remember, you have to stare, de-focus your eyes, and then chant. That could be asking too much. And if you don't have absolute privacy, forget it.

If you feel that you must chant to help you form the cloud, use the mantra RA-MA, which is the name of a Hindu god and the name of a city where the School of Prophets was founded in ancient Palestine. RA represents the masculine energy. MA is the negative, feminine potency. Together, they are the creative power that brought the universe into existence out of the cloud in the beginning. Draw out each syllable and repeat them 20 or 25 times per session. If it works for you, fine. If you get no results, drop it.

The Secret Key

Patience is the secret key here. Don't be discouraged. It won't happen that you will see a cloud for the first time; it may not happen after scores of times. But it will happen if you stick with it.

What you may see after some good effort is something that looks like heat waves. That is nothing more than a slight discoloration of the atmosphere.

If your backdrop is white, you may assume you are getting results when you see a faint blue stain. One thing is certain, when you do achieve results you won't be able to see anything on the other side of the cloud.

Step five includes building the cloud. You do this by starting with your hands about a foot or so apart. Then bring them together. Think that you are compressing astral material between your hands. You bring your hands together and then separate them much like a man playing an accordion. This technique may work for you, and if it does you are likely to see balls of light between your hands. If it doesn't, try another technique.

One that you may be successful with concerns will power and eye movement. Your hands are not involved. Once the cloud has started to form, look away from it. Permit the energy to collect in another region of space. After a moment, bring your eyes gradually toward the center, where the main cloud is forming. While you are doing this, command your will power to force the energy in other parts of the room to join with the energy already in the cloud. You can glance up above the cloud and will that the energy up there come down and unite with the energy in the cloud. Do the same by glancing below the cloud, and to either side of it. Above all, do not strain your eyes.

It's not necessary. In fact, your eyes should be passive. All of what you do must be mental.

When you become efficient with this technique you can incorporate step five with step two, which means you can start the building-up process at the same time that you are beginning the concentration that permits the cloud to build in the first place. Doing both steps at the same time helps to relieve the tedium which too often accompanies occult experimentation.

In his definitive work Steve Richards notes that you will probably have some trouble with your cloud after it has formed. It will have a tendency to scatter to the four corners of the room. This is natural and is in accordance with the law of thermodynamics. If you allow it to happen, all the energy in the cloud will become evenly dispersed throughout the room. The action of being dispersed takes the form of a spin. To prevent that from happening, a counter spin must be produced. The dispersing spin is always in a clockwise direction. What you must do is will it to turn in a counterclockwise direction. What will happen then is that the cloud will become smaller and denser. At this point it's suggested that you alternate this step with step five, building more energy into the cloud as you succeed in getting the cloud to spin in a counterclockwise direction. Combining step five with step six will likely give you an incredibly dense cloud. Using this method, some experts have been able to block out the light of a 150-watt bulb. The method has also been compared with forming a nebulae in outer space. Galaxies are allegedly forming this way, with huge clouds spinning and condensing until they form planets.

At this point Richards says you are now ready to make yourself invisible—with the help of your cloud, of course. We will assume that you have a definite cloud with lots of astral substance in it. You must now draw the cloud around you so that you will be invisible. The cloud has to be big enough to completely cover you.

There may be a shine to the cloud. You don't want that because the shine is like a light. What you want is something neutral, something that will blend with your background. Use your will power for this. The shine can be suppressed.

When the large cloud has enshrouded you, look into the mirror to see if you see your reflection. If you don't see it, you have done it!

Into The "Quiet"

It is quite possible to make yourself invisible without producing a mist or cloud, but it is said to be harder to accomplish the "vanishing act" with such methodology simply because most of us do not possess such advanced powers of concentration.

Madame David-Neel in her book *Magic and Mystery in Tibet* explained that if you walk among crowds shouting and bumping into people you will make yourself quite visible. But if you walk noiselessly, touching no one, looking at no one, you may be able to pass without being seen. Animals do this all the time to catch prey. It has also been pointed out that if you sit motionless you can cut down on your visibility. But there is one drawback to this method. Your mind generated disquietness. David-Neel says, "The work of your mind generates an energy which spreads all around the one who produces it, and this energy is felt in various ways by those who come into touch with it."

The idea is to cut off that source of energy, or noise. If you can do that you become as silent as anyone can be. You may still be seen. That is, a camera or mirror would pick up your image, but you would not be noticed.

Said one expert: "When the mind inhibits emanation of its radioactivity it ceases to be the source of mental stimuli to others, so that they become unconscious of the presence of an Adept of the Art, just as they are unconscious of invisible beings living in a rate of vibration unlike their own."

Aleister Crowley wrote: "The real secret of invisibility is not concerned with the laws of optics at all. The trick is to prevent people noticing you when they would normally do so."

Apparently, Crowley had the power to keep people from noticing him. In an experiment, he took a walk along a street dressed in a golden crown and a scarlet robe. He did not attract attention to himself.

Eliphas Levi points out: "A man, for example, pursued by murderers, after having run down a side street, returns instantly and comes, with a calm face, toward those who are pursing him, or mixes with them and appears occupied with the same pursuit. He will certainly render himself invisible....The person who would be seen is always remarked, and he who would remain unnoticed effaces himself and disappears."

A Simple Method

Sit quietly. Close your eyes. Allow your consciousness to slowly turn inward. Believe it or not, this does not require any effort. It's a natural and involuntary process. The first is to blot out your environment. Make yourself oblivious to it. Next, keep in your mind the thought that you want to hide. Do this even though you may be sitting in an open room with other people around. Finally, eliminate all thoughts from your mind. That's not hard to do because you do that, generally, every night when you go to sleep.

The first step may be easy for you if you have ever meditated. In that situation you do eliminate your environment. The last part may be the hardest. Driving all thoughts from your mind, while being fully awake, is difficult for some. Only the Adepts can stop it completely.

But remember, thoughts produce energy, and energy makes you more visible. Stop thinking, remain motionless with eyes closed, and you become invisible. Not in the literal sense of the word, but unnoticed.

J.H. Brennan has devised a method to stop thought-energy. He says that if he cannot stop himself from shouting, he can conceal himself from you by surrounding himself with a sound-proof screen that shuts out the noise. He uses the word "shouting" to mean "thinking." There is a technique for doing that and it is taught by the AMORC Rosicrucians. It is called the "veil of invisibility."

The Veil of Invisibility

With this technique you can actually produce real invisibility. The Rosicrucians advise you to sit quietly as though you are meditating. Close your eyes. Now imagine that you are completely surrounded by a soundproof siren. Think of it as a certain hanging down all around you, completely concealing you. Think of the curtain until you can feel its presence, keeping in mind that the curtain will make you invisible to others.

How can you tell if your experiment is successful? Simple. Place a mirror at the opposite side of the room, beyond the Veil's influence. You will be able to see through the curtain, but outsiders will not be able to see in. If you are successful, you will not see your image in the mirror.

But don't hope for success immediately. Give yourself plenty of time to achieve it. Be patient—and never become discouraged. Acquiring occult powers is not easy. You can be sure that those who are successful are those who have enormous patience.

CIA & KGB

Apparently, the CIA and KGB have combined a variety of methods. A PSI Corps was actually formed in Washington some time ago, and is made up of at least 1,000 super psychics who are kept on "The Company" payroll to find out the top secrets of our most hated enemies. Up until recently, this PSI Corps was free to keep tabs on the Soviet high command in an attempt to discover the next moves of the communist military. Can you imagine what secrets could be learned if CIA spies were able to move about undetected behind Kremlin walls? From word that has leaked out of a more liberal Russia as of late, it seems that the KGB was also utilizing their own "mystic masters" to become invisible to spy on various American installations abroad.

Going to the movies may be an adventure to many, but the science fiction-like powers displayed in *Total Recall* and in other mind bending motion pictures are no longer just possible in the world of special effects. Controlling minds, altering states of consciousness, and even becoming invisible, are abilities more and more people are learning to deal with.

NOTICE: This special report is adapted from the forthcom-

JOURNEY TO DIMENSIONS
NEVER BEFORE EXPERIENCED!
BRAD STEIGER
ALTERED STATES AWARENESS TAPES

Come with America's leading authority on the New Age and explore the fascinating universe most of us know so little about. Here are audio cassette tapes that are based upon Brad Steiger's perfect seminars and workshops which have touched the hearts and minds of thousands of men and women actively seeking thoughts and ideas to improve their lives and make our planet a better place on which to live.

Each Brad Steiger Awareness Tape is approximately one full hour in length and represents the most beautiful listening pleasure you will ever experience. These tapes have been designed especially to reprogram your body, mind, and spirit to a higher state of being and open your channels to higher intelligence. These are tapes you will want to listen to over and over again. They will place you into a tranquil state of mind. They will relax you and make you feel as if you are one with the Universe. These tapes are like no other...they are a unique experience that you will want to share with all those you love.

1. <u>THE HEALING LIGHT</u>

The Universe exists to do our biding; nothing in the cosmos has been created by chance. The Healing Light serves a very therapeutic purpose...it can enrich our lives and it can also be used to heal both ourselves and others. This is the famous technique described in Brad Steiger's *Minds Through Space and Time*. After describing the essence of his method, Brad then places you into an altered state of consciousness so that you might direct the Healing Light into your own life and experience a multitude of benefits.

2. GOOD HEALTH THROUGH COLOR THERAPY

Every color of the spectrum has its place in keeping the human mind and body in perfect attunement. Now you can learn what the colors represent and how they can be used to balance out your existence. You will find this Awareness Tape to be relaxing, helpful and refreshingly positive. This material has helped many others to walk in perfect harmony and is useful in ridding the system of anxiety and fears, as well as a variety of aches and pains.

3. COSMIC VISION QUEST

Journey with Brad Steiger as he induces you into an extremely altered state of consciousness and prepares you to receive your own vision teachings. You are taken to the Timeless Realm to receive your own personal visions of the Soul's relationship to the cosmos, other intelligences in the universe, the beginning of human life on this planet, your most important past life, and your mission on Earth.

4. USING DREAMS TO SHAPE A MORE POSITIVE LIFE

Inner Alchemist, practitioner of American Indian Medicine and Hawaiian Huna, Brad Steiger has long used his dreams to shape his waking reality. In this valuable awareness tape he will teach you how to create your own reality and shape a more positive life through control of your dreams.

5. EXPERIENCE PAST LIFE RECALL

Have you ever experienced fleeting memories of a life in the distant past? Would you like to know who you might have been in a prior incarnation? Is there something troubling you in this life which may be the result of a past life episode? If you believe in reincarnation let Brad Steiger take you back so that you can explore the dusty pages of your subconscious and apply what you learn in this altered state of consciousness to better your current life situation.

6. BECOME A SPIRITUAL ALCHEMIST

Discover your "true self" and learn how to use the marvelous universal energy that exists within us all in order to achieve self-mastery and to work miracles. Listen to sounds of an enchanted kingdom and let Brad Steiger raise your consciousness so that it will become possible to transform your life from an ordinary one to one that is a treasure of gold. This tape truly represents the most beautiful hour of listening pleasure you will ever experience and has been designed to re-program your body, mind and spirit to a higher state of being and open your channels to higher intelligences.

7. CREATING A CLOSE ENCOUNTER & E.T. SITUATION

Have you ever wanted to see a UFO or experience a close encounter with an extraterrestrial being?

Now Brad Steiger has created a creative visualization that may enable you to fashion a remarkable encounter or recall an ET experience that has been buried in your past. This is the tape for all those who have ever had "missing time" or dreamed the "impossible."

8. PAST LIVES THRU SOUL CONTACT

On side one of this Awareness Tape you will meet your "higher self" who will introduce you to your Karmic-counterpart during the lifetime or lifetimes that most directly affect your present life on Earth. You'll discover why you have come together with certain individuals from your past life or lives. On side two you will discover your true mission. You will learn why you first chose to come to Earth. What it is you are to do here.

9. CREATING A POSITIVE APPROACH TO LIFE'S PROBLEMS

Brad Steiger teaches you how to eliminate fear and negativity from your life. A remarkable technique utilizing the

Violet Light of Transmutation permits you to dissolve negativity whenever it threatens you.

This is the tape you should use if you feel you are coming under psychic attack or need protection against negative forces.

10. DISCOVERING YOUR SPIRIT TEACHER

Everyone of us has one or more spirit guides whose purpose is to guide your life so that we can take advantage of our full potential. Now Brad Steiger takes you along on a journey to contact your teacher from a higher spiritual plane and permits you to enrich your life through the promise of an on-going relationship with your own spirit teacher.

11. THE DIVINE FIRE

On this Awareness Tape you will experience the power of becoming your own Guru and will undergo the feeling of transfer of thought, spirit and power from higher intelligences. Everyone is a potential mystic.

12. EXPLORING FUTURE LIVES

You can zip across space and time and explore a future life situation, returning to the present time with vital insights which will assist you.

13. THE STARBIRTH ODYSSEY (WITH FRANCES PASCAL STEIGER) DOUBLE TAPE—LENGTH: 120 MIN.

Get ready for an experience like no other. Find out if you are a STARPERSON. learn how to evaluate your position on the spiritual path and what awareness you have accumulated to date on this planet.

NEW TAPES—JUST RELEASED

14. MASTERING THE ART OF ASTRAL PROJECTION

Learn several techniques that enable you to leave your

body just as the great mystics throughout history have done.

15. INDIAN MEDICINE WHEEL
Hold your own "Vision Quest," communicate with Earth spirits. Authentic music and chants.

16. BRAD STEIGER'S CRYSTAL MEDITATION
Invoke powers meditating with crystals that lead to spiritual growth & personal blessings.

HOW TO ORDER

Clip out the coupon below, checking off the corresponding numbers of the tapes you wish to order. Or you may write the titles on a sheet of paper. Tape prices are as follows: 1 tape—$9.95; 3 tapes—$25; 6 tapes—$40. All 17 tapes—$100. Please note that STARBIRTH ODYSSEY counts as two tapes. Add for postage and handling $1.50 for the first 3 tapes, or $2.50 if your order is for more than 3 tapes.

- -

INNER LIGHT, Box 753, New Brunswick, NJ 08903
Please send me the following tape(s) listed by number:

❑ 1   ❑ 2   ❑ 3   ❑ 4   ❑ 5   ❑ 6   ❑ 7   ❑ 8   ❑ 9

❑ 10   ❑ 11   ❑ 12   ❑ 13   ❑ 14   ❑ 15   ❑ 16

Name _____

Address _____

City, State, Zip _____

NOTE: NJ residents must add sales tax. Allow 4–6 weeks for delivery. Canadian & foreign customers add $3 payable in U.S. funds by check drawn on a U.S. bank.